Who Am Eye Devotional

30 Days of Discovering Your Identity in Christ

Dr. Johan Green

Who Am Eye Devotional - 30 Days of Discovering Your Identity in Christ
From Confusion to Clarity About Whose You Are

Published by Learn Live Hope Journey LLC
www.learnlivehopejourney.info

Printed in the United States of America

First Edition: 2025

Contents

Acknowledgements

First, I thank my mother, **Alice**. You have been my faithful proofreader and fierce editor—often in seasons when your own health was fragile. Your steadfast love, honest feedback, and brave endurance shaped every page of this devotional and shaped me more deeply as a **person, father, and pastor**. I am a better man because of your courage and your love.

I give all glory to the **Holy Spirit** for His abiding presence. From first sentence to final edit, He guided my thoughts, slowed my pace, corrected my heart, and breathed life into these reflections.

And to you, dear reader: I have prayed for you while writing—prayed for **identity formation in Christ** and for **healing in your soul**. May these pages become a gentle companion on your walk with the **LORD** and with His people. May the Spirit anchor you in your **True Self in Christ**, and may grace meet you in every step.

With gratitude and hope,
Dr. Johan Green

Introduction

Welcome to Your Identity Journey

The Question That Changes Everything

There's a question I've been asking most of my life: "Who am I?"

Maybe you're asking it too. Maybe you've asked it in moments of success when you wondered if your achievements really define you. Maybe you've asked it in moments of failure when everything you thought you were, seemed to crumble. Maybe you're asking it right now, holding this devotional, wondering if 30 days can really make a difference.

Here's what I've discovered through my own journey and years of walking with others through theirs: **The question "Who am I?" will exhaust you until you learn to ask "Whose am I?" instead.**

This devotional series is designed to guide you through that transformation—from the exhausting search for self-definition to the liberating discovery of divine belonging.

My Story: From Sidewalk to Sanctuary

I'll never forget standing on a sidewalk, watching friends drive past without acknowledging me. I had just lost everything—my business, my home, my reputation. In that moment, stripped of every external marker of identity, I asked God the question that would change my life: "Lord, who am I?"

I was no longer the successful businessman. I was no longer the guy with the title. I was just Johan—barefoot in identity, standing on nothing but grace.

What I didn't know then was that I was exactly where I needed to be, for God to begin His deepest work. That devastating loss became the doorway to discovering my truest identity—not in what I did, but in whose I am.

How This Devotional Works

This is **Devotional 1** of a three-part series based on my book *Who Am Eye?* Over the next 30 days, you'll journey through the first four chapters, discovering:

Week 1 (Days 1-7): How to listen to God's voice above all others

Week 2 (Days 8-14): How your body reveals which version of yourself is leading

Week 3 (Days 15-21): How your soul processes life and identity

Week 4 (Days 22-28): How your spirit anchors you in whose you are

Days 29-30: Integration and new beginning

What Makes This Different

This isn't just another devotional to read and forget. Each day includes:

Scripture Foundation - God's Word as your anchor

Reflection - Personal stories and theological depth

Guided Questions - Space for honest self-discovery

Bible Character Reflection - Learning from those who've walked this path

Spiritual Practice - Daily exercises that transform knowledge into experience

Prayer - Authentic conversation with your Heavenly Father

Daily Declaration - Truth to carry with you

The Four Selves Framework

Throughout this journey, you'll encounter references to the **Four Selves**—a framework for understanding the different versions of yourself that show up depending on circumstances:

Actual Self: The honest, messy reality of being human

False Self: The wounded you, operating from fear and pain

Presentable Self: The curated you, managing impressions

True Self: The Christ-formed self, secure in God's love

You'll learn to recognize which self is leading in different situations and how to live more consistently from your True Self.

How to Use This Devotional

Daily Commitment: Set aside 15-20 minutes each day in a quiet place where you won't be interrupted.

Weekly Pattern:

Days 1-6: New teachings and practices

Day 7: Sacred pause for integration and reflection

What You'll Need:

This devotional

A journal or the space provided

An open heart

Willingness to be honest with God and yourself

Transformation is not an event—it's a journey. Some days you'll experience breakthrough. Other days you'll struggle to feel anything at all. Both are normal. Both are part of the process.

The goal isn't perfection. The goal is **progression**—learning day by day to recognize God's voice, honor the temple He's given you, understand how your soul processes life, and anchor yourself in the spirit's communion with Him.

What Comes Next

This is Devotional 1 of 3. After completing these 30 days:

Devotional 2 will guide you through Chapters 5-8 (Understanding Your Selves, Emotions, Relationships, and Wounds)

Devotional 3 will complete the journey through Chapters 9-12 (The Sacred Threshold, Breaking Free from Lies, and Reclaiming Your Identity)

You can choose to continue immediately or take time to integrate what you've learned before moving forward. This is your journey—honor your own pace.

My Prayer for You

Father, I lift up every person holding this devotional right now. You know their story—their wounds, their questions, their deepest longings. Meet them in these pages. Speak louder than their doubts. Break through the noise that's been drowning out Your voice. Over the next 30 days, remind them whose they are. Not because of what they've done, but because of what You've done. Transform them from the inside out. In Jesus' name, amen.

Let's Begin

You are not here by accident. God has been speaking your name since before you were born. The question is: Are you ready to learn to hear it?

Welcome to the beginning of everything.

Dr. Johan Green

Week 1: Listen To Hear The Heart (Chapter 1)

Day 1 – I Have Always Known You

WHO GOD SAYS I AM

Scripture

"Before I formed you in the womb I knew you, and before you were born I consecrated you; I have appointed you as a prophet to the nations."
—Jeremiah 1:5 (AMP)

Reflection

When I first encountered this verse, I was navigating one of the most disorienting seasons of my life. I had just gone through a difficult divorce, and my identity felt lost in the fog of pain, shame, and transition.

But here's what I didn't realize at the time: **I was asking the right question ("Who am I?") while listening to all the wrong voices for the answer.**

The world's voice said: *Failure. Divorced. Disqualified.*

My wound's voice said: *Not enough. Never will be.*

My performance voice said: *Work harder. Prove yourself. Maybe then you'll matter.*

It was in that broken moment, sitting alone with my Bible and my questions, that I heard a whisper in my spirit—not loud, but unmistakable: *"You are not who the world says you are. You are who I say you are."*

It was the voice of the Holy Spirit—and it changed everything.

Here's the truth that will anchor this entire week: God has been speaking over you since before you were born. The question isn't whether He's speaking—it's whether you've learned to recognize His voice above all the others.

Listening Practice: Whose Voice Is This?

Today, I want you to notice something. When thoughts about your identity arise, **pause and ask: "Whose voice is speaking this thought?"**

Is it:

The voice of a **past wound** (shame, rejection, failure)?

The voice of **others' opinions** (what they said, what they think)?

The voice of **your own critic** (performance pressure, comparison)?

Or the voice of **your Heavenly Father** (truth, love, calling)?

God's voice always sounds like love—even when it's corrective. His voice reminds you that you are chosen, known, consecrated, and called. His voice doesn't change based on your performance. His voice has been speaking your true name since before you could hear it.

Let today be the day you begin to **tune your spiritual ears** to the voice that matters most.

Guided Questions for Reflection

What labels have you been carrying that God never gave you? (Examples: "Failure," "Too much," "Not enough," "Damaged goods")

....

....

Whose voice first spoke those labels over you? (Be specific—a parent, a failure, a betrayal, a comparison)

....

....

What does God's voice say about you in this Scripture?

....

....

Bible Character Reflection

Jeremiah – God spoke this word over Jeremiah when he was young and feeling unqualified. Jeremiah's immediate response? "I do not know how to speak, for I am only a youth" (v.6).

Notice what God did: He didn't argue with Jeremiah's feelings. He simply **spoke truth louder** than Jeremiah's self-doubt. God said, "Do not say, 'I am only a youth'... I am with you" (v.7-8).

The lesson: Your feelings about yourself are real, but they don't determine truth. God's voice does.

Spiritual Practice: Sacred Listening (5 minutes)

Find a quiet place. Sit comfortably. Close your eyes.

Breathe – Three deep breaths. With each exhale, release one false label you've carried.

Listen – In silence, ask: "Father, what have You been saying about me that I haven't been listening to?"

Receive – Don't force it. If a thought comes that sounds like love, write it down. If nothing comes, that's okay—you're training your ears.

Declare – Speak this aloud: "I am chosen. I am loved. I am known. I am not alone."

Note: If this feels awkward or nothing happens, that's normal. You're developing a muscle you may not have used before. Keep practicing.

Prayer

Holy Spirit, I invite You into this journey of rediscovering who I am. Silence the lies spoken over me and replace them with Your truth. Teach me to recognize Your voice—not just intellectually, but in my heart. I am not forgotten—I am known, loved, and chosen by You. Let me walk today with confidence in who You say I am. In Jesus' name, amen.

Daily Declaration

I am not what I've done.

I am not what others have said.

I am who God says I am—
and He's been saying it since before I was born.

Connection to Chapter 1

Today's practice of distinguishing voices directly connects to Chapter 1's teaching: **"The greatest discoveries in life don't come through**

achievement—they come through surrender." You're surrendering your need to define yourself and learning to listen for the voice that has always known who you are.

Tomorrow, we'll go deeper into what it sounds like when God speaks truth over your identity.

Day 2 – Learning to Recognize the Father's Voice

Who God Says I Am

Scripture

"See what an incredible quality of love the Father has shown to us, that we would [be permitted to] be named, called and counted the children of God! And so we are."
—1 John 3:1 (AMP)

"Speak, Lord, for thy servant heareth."
—1 Samuel 3:9 (KJV)

Reflection

Yesterday, you learned that God has been speaking over you since before you were born. Today, we address the harder question: **How do you recognize His voice when so many other voices are shouting for your attention?**

I remember sitting in my car one morning, emotionally exhausted after a difficult counseling session. Multiple voices were competing in my head:

Pain's voice said: "You're a failure. You'll never figure this out."

People's voice said: "You should be further along by now."

Performance voice said: "Work harder. Prove you're worth keeping."

In that chaos, I leaned my head on the steering wheel and said aloud, "God, I feel like a stranger to myself."

And then came the voice I almost missed because it was so different from the others. It was quiet, gentle, but unmistakable: **"You are My child."**

Not "Try harder." Not "You've disappointed Me." Not "Earn your way back." Just... "You are My child."

That's how the Father's voice sounds—it reminds you whose you are, not what you've done.

The Samuel Principle: Learning to Listen

In Chapter 1, we explored young Samuel's story. He heard a voice calling his name in the night, but he kept running to Eli because **he had not yet recognize God's voice** (1 Samuel 3:7).

Notice what happened: Samuel wasn't spiritually immature or unfaithful. He simply hadn't learned to distinguish God's voice from other familiar voices yet. He assumed the voice must be coming from someone he already knew.

We do the same thing. When we hear thoughts about our identity, we often assume they're coming from:

Our past (wounds speaking)

Our fears (anxiety speaking)

Our performance (pressure speaking)

But Eli taught Samuel the key to recognition: **"Speak, Lord, for thy servant heareth"** (1 Samuel 3:9). Not "Speak if You're there" or "Speak so I can evaluate You." Simply: **"I'm listening. I'm ready to hear You as my Lord."**

How to Distinguish the Father's Voice

Here's what I've learned about recognizing God's voice versus the other voices that compete for our attention:

The Father's Voice:

Calls you "child" even when you feel like a failure

Brings conviction without condemnation

Speaks truth wrapped in love

Points you toward who you're becoming, not just what you've done

Creates peace, even when the truth is hard

Reminds you of your belovedness before addressing your behavior

Pain's Voice (False Self):

Calls you by your wounds: "damaged," "rejected," "not enough"

Brings shame and hopelessness

Replays your failures on repeat

Keeps you stuck in the past

Creates anxiety and despair

Performance Voice (Presentable Self):

Calls you by your productivity: "useful," "successful," "impressive"

Brings exhaustion from constant striving

Measures your worth by what you accomplish

Creates comparison and competition

Never lets you rest

The Father calls you "child"—and that identity goes deeper than your scars, titles, or even your best moments.

The Holy Pause: Practicing Recognition

Chapter 1 teaches that transformation requires learning to pause before reacting. Today, I want you to practice what I call **the Recognition Pause:**

When a thought about your identity arises (especially a negative one), don't immediately accept it or fight it. Instead:

Pause – Take three deep breaths

Ask – "Whose voice is this? Does this sound like my Father?"

Test – "Does this bring shame or conviction? Hopelessness or hope?"

Listen – "Father, what are YOU saying about this?"

This isn't about positive thinking—it's about **training your spiritual ears to recognize the Shepherd's voice** (John 10:27).

Guided Questions for Reflection

What voice has been speaking loudest about your identity lately? (Be specific—is it a past wound, a current fear, others' opinions, or your Heavenly Father?)

....

....

How does that voice make you feel? (Anxious? Exhausted? Peaceful? Loved? Condemned?)

....

....

What name or label are you still carrying that contradicts God's truth that you are His child?

....

....

Practice the Recognition Pause right now: Father, what are YOU saying about who I am? (Write what comes—even if it's just silence. Silence can be God giving you space to stop performing and just BE His child.)

....

....

Bible Character Reflection

Mephibosheth – Once a royal son, he became crippled and forgotten, living in a place called Lo Debar (literally "place of no pasture"—a wasteland). When King David called him by name and restored his place at the royal table, Mephibosheth couldn't believe it: "What is your servant, that you should notice a dead dog like me?" (2 Samuel 9:8).

Notice David's response: He didn't argue with Mephibosheth's feelings about himself. He simply kept calling him to the table. Day after day, the king's voice spoke louder than Mephibosheth's shame.

Your lesson: Like Samuel learning to recognize God's voice, and like Mephibosheth learning to hear the king's invitation above his own shame, **you are learning to let the Father's voice drown out every other voice that tries to define you.**

Spiritual Practice: The Recognition Exercise (10 minutes)

Part 1: Identify the Voices (5 minutes)

Write down one negative thought you've had about yourself recently. Then trace it:

When did I first hear this message?

Whose voice originally spoke this over me?

How has this voice shaped my choices?

Part 2: Invite the Father's Voice (5 minutes)

Now sit quietly and pray: *"Speak, Lord, for Your servant is listening. What do YOU say about this?"*

Wait. Don't rush. If a thought comes that sounds like love and truth, write it down.

Part 3: Visual Reminder

Write the word **"CHILD"** on a piece of paper. Tape it somewhere you'll see today—your bathroom mirror, steering wheel, or desk. Every time you see it, practice the Recognition Pause:

"I am a child of God. That's what my Father calls me. I am loved, secure, and accepted—not because of what I do, but because of whose I am."

Prayer

Father, thank You for calling me Your child. Teach me to recognize Your voice above every other voice competing for my attention. When pain's voice shouts shame, let me hear Your whisper of love. When performance pressure screams "not enough," let me hear Your declaration: "You are Mine." Help me shed every false label and walk boldly in the truth of who I am. I'm learning to listen, Father. Speak—Your child is here. In Jesus' name, amen.

Daily Declaration

I am a child of God.
I am learning to recognize my Father's voice.
His voice calls me beloved—
and that's louder than every other voice combined.

Connection to Chapter 1

Today's practice builds directly on Chapter 1's teaching: **"The journey of identity is not about constructing something new—it's about uncovering what's already there."** God has been calling you "child" all along. You're simply learning to recognize His voice above the noise.

Tomorrow, we'll explore what happens when you finally believe what the Father has been saying.

Quote of the Day

"You don't need a title to be worthy—you only need a Father who calls you by name... and the spiritual ears to recognize His voice."

Day 3 – Learning to Listen to Yourself Honestly

WHO GOD SAYS I AM

Scripture

"But you are a chosen race, a royal priesthood, a consecrated nation, a [special] people for God's own possession, so that you may proclaim the excellencies [the wonderful deeds and virtues] of Him who called you out of darkness into His marvelous light."
—1 Peter 2:9 (AMP)

"Why are you cast down, O my soul, and why are you in turmoil within me? Hope in God; for I shall again praise him, my salvation and my God."
—Psalm 42:5 (ESV)

Reflection

There's a verse I return to often that captures something profound about identity: **"Why are you cast down, O my soul?"** (Psalm 42:5)

Notice what David does here—he **talks to his soul**. He listens to what's happening inside him, acknowledges it honestly, and then redirects his hope toward God. This is the practice we're developing this week: learning to listen honestly to ourselves so we can hear God clearly.

Here's what I've discovered: **You cannot proclaim the truth of 1**

Peter 2:9 ("you are chosen") if you won't first acknowledge the voices inside you that whisper "you are ordinary."

There was a time in my life when I felt completely forgotten in the crowd. Like nothing I offered could make a meaningful difference. I believed the lie that being faithful in small things didn't matter much in God's kingdom.

But here's what I was doing wrong: **I was trying to believe I was "chosen" while refusing to acknowledge the voice inside me that felt completely ordinary.**

I would read "You are a royal priesthood" and think, "I should feel different. What's wrong with me that I don't?" But I never actually **listened** to what my soul was trying to tell me about why I felt that way.

The Missing Practice: Listening to Your Actual Self

Chapter 1 of *Who Am Eye?* teaches that your **Actual Self** is "the beautiful, messy reality of being human—you without filters, acknowledging both your brokenness and your belovedness."

Before you can consistently live from the truth that you're chosen, you need to practice **honest listening to what's actually happening in your soul**. Not to stay there, but to bring it to God.

Here's the practice David models in Psalm 42:

He listens to his soul honestly: "Why are you cast down, O my soul?"

He doesn't shame himself for the turmoil: He acknowledges it

He then redirects his hope: "Hope in God"

This is the rhythm: **Listen → Acknowledge → Redirect**

Why This Matters for Identity

Many of us try to skip the "listening and acknowledging" part. We jump straight to declaration: "I am chosen! I am royal!" But when the feelings of being ordinary return (and they will), we assume something's wrong with us for not "feeling chosen enough."

But God's not asking you to deny your feelings—He's asking you to bring them to Him honestly.

When I finally sat with my feelings of being forgotten and ordinary, and brought them honestly to God, something shifted. Instead of Him saying, "Stop feeling that way," He said: **"Tell Me more. Why do you feel forgotten?"**

And as I talked to Him about it—really listened to my own heart and let Him listen too—I realized I'd been measuring my significance by how visible I was, how much I accomplished, how many people noticed me.

That's when the truth of being "chosen" could finally sink in. Not because I forced myself to believe it, but because I let God address the actual lie underneath my feelings.

The "Tell Me More" Prayer in Practice

Today, I want you to practice what Chapter 1 calls the **"Tell Me More"** prayer—but directed at yourself first, then with God.

Step 1: Listen to Your Soul (3 minutes)

Ask yourself: "When I read 'You are chosen,' what voice inside me resists that truth?"

Write honestly:

"I feel ordinary because..."

"I feel unqualified because..."

"I feel forgotten because..."

Don't filter. Don't spiritualize yet. Just listen.

Step 2: Bring It to God (3 minutes)

Now pray: "Father, I've been feeling ____________. Tell me more about what You see when You look at this feeling."

Wait. Listen. Write what comes.

Step 3: Redirect with Truth (2 minutes)

Now—after listening honestly to yourself and to God—you can authentically declare: "Even though I feel ________, the truth You speak over me is: I am chosen."

This isn't denial. This is **anchoring your hope in truth while acknowledging your reality.**

Guided Questions for Reflection

What feeling or thought about yourself have you been trying to ignore or "pray away" instead of honestly listening to it?

....

....

If you were to ask that feeling "Tell me more—why are you here?" what would it say?

(Example: "I feel ordinary because I compare myself to others" or "I feel forgotten because my dad never affirmed me")

....

....

Practice the "Tell Me More" prayer right now: Father, what do YOU see when You look at this feeling I've been carrying?

....

....

How does knowing you are "chosen" speak to the specific feeling you just acknowledged?

....

....

Bible Character Reflection

David (Psalm 42) – Notice David's honesty: "My tears have been my food day and night" (v.3). He doesn't pretend. He doesn't perform spiritual maturity. He listens to his soul's turmoil and brings it before God.

But then notice the shift: "Why are you cast down, O my soul?... Hope in God" (v.5). He doesn't stay in the feeling, but he doesn't skip over it either. **He listens, acknowledges, then redirects.**

Esther – A young Jewish girl living in exile, she never imagined she would be queen. But here's what many miss about Esther's story: when Mordecai told her she was chosen "for such a time as this" (Esther 4:14), **she was terrified** (v.11).

She didn't immediately feel chosen or brave. She felt ordinary and afraid. But she practiced what we're learning: she **acknowledged her fear honestly** ("If I perish, I perish" - v.16), **then acted from her true identity** anyway.

Spiritual Practice: The Honest Mirror (10 minutes)

Part 1: The Honest Conversation (5 minutes)

Stand in front of a mirror. Look at yourself. Ask aloud:

"What have I been afraid to tell God about how I really feel about myself?"

Then answer honestly. Out loud. Let yourself hear your own voice.

Part 2: Invite God Into the Honesty (3 minutes)

Now ask: "Father, I've just told You the truth about how I feel. What do YOU want to say about this?"

Listen. If a thought comes that sounds like love, write it down.

Part 3: The Declaration (2 minutes)

Now—after the honesty—write these three affirmations and speak them over yourself:

"I am royalty in God's kingdom—even when I feel ordinary"

"I have a purpose that brings light—even when I can't see it yet"

"I am not disqualified by my past—God chose me knowing everything"

Notice the difference? You're **not denying the feeling—you're declaring truth that's bigger than the feeling.**

Prayer

Father, thank You that You're for not being afraid of my honesty. Thank You for being able to bring You the messy, unfiltered truth about how I feel, and You don't shame me for it. Today I'm learning to listen—really listen—to what my soul is trying to tell me, so I can bring it to You. Help me see myself through Your eyes—as chosen, holy, and set apart—not by denying my struggles, but by letting Your truth speak louder. Teach me to hope in You, even when my soul feels cast down. In Jesus' name, amen.

Daily Declaration

I am chosen—not because I feel it every moment,
but because God spoke it over me before I could earn or lose it.
Today I practice listening honestly to my soul,
so I can hear His voice more clearly.

Connection to Chapter 1

Today's practice directly applies Chapter 1's teaching: **"The soul is**

where your real story is stored... it's where you wrestle with your deepest questions." Before you can consistently live as "chosen," you must learn to listen to the questions your soul is actually asking—and bring them honestly to the Father who calls you His own.

Tomorrow, we'll explore what happens when you stop performing and start resting in your identity.

Quote of the Day

"God doesn't just forgive our story—He listens to it first, then repurposes it for royalty."

Day 4 – Learning to Listen in Relationships

WHO GOD SAYS I AM

Scripture

"The Spirit Himself testifies and confirms together with our spirit [assuring us] that we [believers] are children of God."

—Romans 8:16 (AMP)

"Know this, my beloved brothers: let every person be quick to hear, slow to speak, slow to anger."

—James 1:19 (ESV)

Reflection

Here's something that completely changed how I experience God's voice: **The way I listen to people directly affects how I listen to God.**

Chapter 1 of *Who Am Eye?* teaches this crucial truth: "When we learn to listen well in our human relationships, it transforms how we listen to God. When we can't feel our own pain, we often can't fully experience joy, intimacy, or God's comfort."

I learned this lesson the hard way as a father.

For years, I struggled with anxiety and fear during my early ministry years. But what I didn't realize was that my inability to listen to my own emotional experience was also affecting how I listened to my children—and ultimately, how I heard God's voice over my identity.

There came a defining day when I took my boys up a mountain—not to speak, but to **listen their souls back into life**. The terrifying step, was asking them to share everything they felt I had failed them in as a father. I promised them no retaliation, no justification, and no defensiveness. They needed to feel safe enough to speak their truth and know they would be heard.

And I listened.

Not to respond. Not to defend. Not to explain. Just to hear them.

Something profound happened on that mountain: **When I finally stopped trying to have the last word and simply created space for my sons to be heard, I learned what the Father had been trying to teach me all along—that He listens to me in the same way.**

The Connection: How We Listen to Others, Reveals How We Hear God

The Holy Spirit testifies with our spirit that we are God's children (Romans 8:16). But here's what I've discovered: **if I can't listen to others without needing to control the conversation, I struggle to hear the Spirit's gentle testimony too.**

Think about it:

If in relationships you:

Need to have the last word → You'll struggle to let God's word be final

Listen only to respond → You'll miss what the Spirit is actually saying

Can't handle others' emotions → You'll numb your own emotions where God wants to speak

Control conversations → You'll try to control your prayer time instead of surrendering

But when you learn to:

Give others space to be heard → You create space to hear God

Listen to understand, not fix → You hear the Spirit's comfort, not just commands

Sit with uncomfortable emotions → You let God meet you in painful places

Practice "Tell me more" with people → You naturally use it with God

Dallas Willard's Wisdom: The Discipline of Not Having the Last Word

Chapter 1 quotes Dallas Willard's teaching that transformed my listening: **not needing to have the last word** is one of the most powerful forms of sacred listening.

Willard teaches that every moment is an opportunity to be with our Teacher. When we practice restraint in conversations—choosing to hear rather than immediately respond—we're actually training ourselves to recognize the Holy Spirit's voice.

I often feel stressed. But I am actually living in the reality of the gospel, when I stop needing to control every outcome, including conversations.

This is why listening to others is spiritual formation for hearing God.

The "Tell Me More" Practice in Relationships

Today's practice is simple but transformative: **Use "Tell me more" with one person.**

This simple phrase—"Tell me more"—can be so powerful. When someone pours out years of emotion in one long sentence, it becomes overwhelming. That's when I guide couples and individuals to slow down: "Let's try one thought at a time." And when that single thought is mirrored back, something sacred happens—the sender feels heard, maybe for the first time.

Here's the practice:

When someone shares something with you today (spouse, child, friend, coworker), instead of:

Offering advice

Sharing your similar experience

Fixing their problem

Defending yourself

Simply say: **"Tell me more."**

Then listen. Really listen. Mirror back what you heard: "So what I'm hearing is..."

Watch what happens—not just in them, but in you. You'll feel something shift. **This is training your soul to listen the way God listens to you.**

How This Connects to Your Identity

When the Holy Spirit testifies with your spirit that you are God's child (Romans 8:16), **it's often through this same kind of listening.**

You bring your pain, your questions, your doubts to God. And instead of immediate answers or fixing, you often hear: **"Tell me more. I'm listening."**

When you practice this with others, you're learning to recognize the Father's listening heart toward you.

I remember unpacking years of trying to earn acceptance—from others, from myself, even from God. What broke me open wasn't condemnation. It was experiencing the Father's **listening presence**: *"Tell me more. I'm not going anywhere. You're My child."*

That quiet assurance from the Holy Spirit came because I had finally learned to stop performing and start listening—both to others and to myself.

Guided Questions for Reflection

When was the last time you truly listened to someone without planning your response while they were talking? What happened?

....

....

Which of your Four Selves typically shows up when listening to others?

False Self: Controls the conversation, needs the last word

Presentable Self: Listens to maintain image, says what people want to hear

Actual Self: Can admit "I don't understand yet, tell me more"

True Self: Listens from love and security, not need

....

....

How does your listening style with others mirror how you listen

(or don't listen) to God?

....

....

Practice right now: If the Holy Spirit said "Tell me more" about something you're carrying, what would you say?

....

....

Bible Character Reflection

John the Beloved – Among the disciples, John described himself as "the one whom Jesus loved." He rested on Christ's chest at the Last Supper (John 13:23).

But notice what that posture required: **silence, receptivity, listening to Jesus' heartbeat.** John didn't demand answers or control the conversation. He simply **positioned himself to listen.**

He learned to listen to Jesus' heart before he could hear Jesus' words. That intimacy—not performance—became his identity.

Like John, when you practice listening to others' hearts (not just their words), you're training yourself to hear God's heart toward you: *You are My beloved child.*

Spiritual Practice: The Listening Experiment (All Day)

Part 1: With One Person (At least 10 minutes today)

Choose one conversation today where you will practice:

"Tell me more" (say it at least three times)

No advice unless asked

Mirror back what you heard: "So what I'm hearing is..."

Notice when you want to interrupt—pause instead

Part 2: With God (5 minutes)

After practicing listening with a person, sit quietly with God:

Put your hand over your heart and say: *"Holy Spirit, I've practiced listening to someone else today. Now I'm practicing listening to You. Tell me more about who You say I am."*

Then wait. Don't fill the silence. Let Him speak—or let the silence itself be His testimony of peace over you.

Part 3: Journal (3 minutes)

Write what you noticed:

How did practicing "Tell me more" with others change the conversation?

What did you hear from God when you gave Him space to speak?

Which Self was leading when you listened well? When you struggled to listen?

Prayer

Holy Spirit, I need Your voice louder than my need to control, fix, or defend. Teach me to listen—really listen—to the people You've placed in my life, because I know that's where I'm learning to hear You too. Remind me again today that I am Your beloved child—not because I have all the answers, but because You've sealed me with love that listens. Let me live not for approval, but from the identity You're testifying to right now: I belong to You. In Jesus' name, amen.

Daily Declaration

I am not abandoned. I am adopted.
I am a child of the Father who listens to my heart.
Today I practice listening to others,
because that's how I'm learning to hear Him.

Connection to Chapter 1

Today's practice directly applies Chapter 1's core teaching: **"Listening is the forgotten gateway to identity."** Before the Spirit can testify with your spirit that you are God's child, you must create the quiet, listening space where that testimony can be heard. And that space is developed through the daily practice of listening well to others.

Tomorrow, we'll explore what happens when you finally stop striving and start resting in the identity God has already spoken over you.

Quote of the Day

"The Spirit doesn't shout to impress you—it whispers to remind you: You belong. But you only hear the whisper when you've learned to stop needing the last word."

Day 5 – When God's Voice Feels Distant

Who God Says I Am

Scripture

"Even before He made the world, God loved us and chose us in Christ to be holy and without fault in His eyes."
—Ephesians 1:4 (NLT)

"Why are you cast down, O my soul, and why are you in turmoil within me? Hope in God; for I shall again praise him."
—Psalm 42:11 (ESV)

Reflection

Let me be honest with you about something I wrestled with for years: **I believed intellectually that God chose me before the foundation of the world, but I didn't feel it. And that gap between knowing and feeling made me wonder if something was wrong with me spiritually.**

Maybe you're experiencing that same disconnect right now. You've read these beautiful truths all week—that you're known, chosen, called, beloved—but when you sit quietly and ask yourself, "Do I really believe this deep in my soul?" the answer is... complicated.

Here's what I've discovered through my own journey and through Chapter 1's teaching on listening: **The gap between head knowledge and heart belief, often exists because we've been numbing the very emotions, where God wants to speak His truth most powerfully.**

Let me explain what I mean.

The Lie of "Just Believe Harder"

For years, when I struggled to feel God's love, well-meaning people would tell me: "You just need to have more faith. Stop doubting and believe what Scripture says."

But here's what nobody told me: **Sometimes the reason we can't hear God's voice of love is because we've shut down the emotional space where that voice speaks.**

Chapter 1 teaches this crucial truth: "When we can't feel our own pain, we often can't fully experience joy, intimacy, or God's comfort."

Think about it—if you've spent years:

Numbing disappointment through busyness

Avoiding rejection by never being vulnerable

Managing anxiety through control

Hiding shame behind performance

Then you've also numbed the channels through which God's love flows to you.

The same emotional shutdown that protects you from pain also blocks you from experiencing the comfort, joy, and deep assurance that "you are chosen."

My Breaking Point: When Truth Finally Became Real

I'll never forget the moment Ephesians 1:4 moved from my head to my heart.

I was sitting in my car after a particularly painful ministry failure. I had just disappointed people I deeply respected. My performing self was screaming: *"You're disqualified. You've proven you're not chosen."*

And for the first time, instead of **numbing that pain** (through distraction, rationalizing, or spiritual platitudes), I let myself **feel it fully**. I wept. I acknowledged the shame. I didn't try to pray it away or quote victory verses at it.

And then, in that raw, undefended moment, I heard the Father's voice clearer than I'd ever heard it before:

"I chose you before this moment. I chose you before this failure. I chose

you before the world began. This pain you're feeling right now—I want to meet you here."

The truth became real when I stopped managing my emotions and started bringing them honestly to God.

The Practice: Emotional Honesty as the Gateway to Hearing God

Today's practice is different from the previous days. Instead of **declaring truth you're trying to believe**, I want you to **acknowledge the gap between what you know and what you feel.**

This is what Chapter 1 calls listening to your **Actual Self**—the beautiful, messy reality of being human, acknowledging both brokenness and belovedness.

Here's the practice:

Step 1: Acknowledge the Gap (3 minutes)

Finish these sentences honestly:

"The truth says I was chosen before the foundation of the world, but I actually feel..."

"When I try to believe God loved me first, the voice that resists says..."

"The emotion I've been avoiding while trying to 'just have faith' is..."

Don't spiritualize yet. Just be honest.

Step 2: Bring the Gap to God (5 minutes)

Now pray with brutal honesty:

"Father, here's the truth: I read that You chose me before the world began, but I don't feel it. I feel __________ instead. I'm not going to pretend or perform right now. I'm bringing You this gap between my head and my heart. Tell me more about what You see in this space."

Then wait. Listen. Don't rush to fix the feeling.

Step 3: Receive What Comes (2 minutes)

If God speaks (through a thought, Scripture, memory, or just peace), write it down.

If nothing comes, that's okay too. Sometimes God's answer is simply: *"Thank you for being honest with Me. Keep bringing Me the real you."*

Why This Matters for Identity

Romans 8:16 says "The Spirit Himself testifies with our spirit that we are children of God."

But notice—the Spirit testifies **with** your spirit, not **instead of** your spirit. That means **your emotional experience matters**. God wants to speak His truth into the actual condition of your soul, not the condition you're pretending to be in.

When you bring God the honest truth about what you're feeling—doubt, disappointment, numbness, confusion—**you create space for the Spirit's testimony to become real, not just theoretical.**

Guided Questions for Reflection

What emotion have you been avoiding or "praying away" while trying to believe you're chosen?

(Examples: disappointment that God didn't come through, anger that He allowed pain, fear that you're not actually loved)

....

....

If you let yourself fully feel that emotion right now without judging it as "bad faith," what would it say?

....

....

Practice the honest prayer: "Father, I believe You chose me before the world began, but help my unbelief. What I'm actually feeling right now is..." (Finish the prayer)

....

....

What would change if you trusted that God wants to meet you in the gap between knowing and feeling, rather than demanding you close that gap before coming to Him?

....

....

Bible Character Reflection

David – Before he was king, he was overlooked by his own father. When the prophet Samuel came to anoint Israel's next king, David's father Jesse didn't even call him in from the fields (1 Samuel 16:11).

The rejection was real. The pain was valid.

But here's what David teaches us: he didn't deny those feelings. Throughout the Psalms, he brings his raw emotions to God—feeling forgotten, abandoned, cast down. **Yet he also declares truth over those feelings:** "Hope in God" (Psalm 42:11).

David shows us the rhythm: **Feel it → Bring it to God → Redirect hope toward truth**

He was chosen by God while still feeling overlooked by his family. **The truth of being chosen didn't erase the pain—it transformed it.**

Spiritual Practice: The Honest Letter (15 minutes)

Part 1: Write to God (10 minutes)

Take out paper and pen. Write a letter to God that begins:

"Father, here's what I need You to know about how I'm really doing with believing I was chosen before the world began..."

Don't edit. Don't perform. Write the truth—including doubts, resistance, numbness, or whatever is actually there.

Part 2: Listen for His Response (5 minutes)

After you've written your honest letter, sit quietly and ask:

"Father, what do You want to say back to me about what I just wrote?"

Write down whatever comes—even if it's just one sentence, or even just peace.

Prayer

Father, thank You that You're not afraid of my honesty. Thank You that I don't have to pretend I feel chosen when I'm struggling to believe it. Today I'm bringing You the gap—the space between what my head knows and what my heart feels. I believe You chose me before the foundation of the world. But help my unbelief. Meet me in this honest place. I'm listening for Your voice, not performing for Your approval. In Jesus' name, amen.

Daily Declaration

I am chosen—even when I don't feel it yet.
God loved me before the world began—
and He's big enough to handle my honest struggle to believe it.

Today I bring Him the truth, not the performance.

Connection to Chapter 1

Today's practice applies Chapter 1's foundational teaching: **"Pain isn't failure—it's information... When you honor your emotional experience by bringing it to God, you create the sacred space where identity is truly discovered."**

The truth that you were chosen before the foundation of the world becomes transformative not when you force yourself to believe it, but when you bring your honest doubt to the Father who chose you anyway.

Tomorrow, we'll explore how to move from knowing you're chosen to living like someone who believes it.

Quote of the Day

"You weren't added to God's plan later—you were written into it from the start. And He's patient enough to meet you in the gap between knowing that truth and feeling it."

Day 6 – When Listening Changes How You Live

Who God Says I Am

Scripture

"You will know the truth, and the truth will set you free." —John 8:32 (AMP)

"Be ye doers of the word, and not hearers only, deceiving yourselves." —James 1:22 (ASV)

Reflection

We've spent five days learning to listen—to God's voice, to the voices competing for your attention, to your own soul's honest condition, to others in relationship, and to the gap between knowing truth and feeling it.

Today, we ask the question that matters most: So what? How does all this listening actually change how you live?

Here's what I've discovered: **Listening isn't the destination—it's the gateway.** Everything we've practiced this week prepares you for what comes next: living from the truth you're learning to hear.

Chapter 1 of *Who Am Eye?* ends with this invitation: "The journey ahead won't always be comfortable, but it will be worth it. Because on the other side of acknowledged pain is authentic freedom."

But here's the key—**you can't get to authentic freedom by skipping**

over the listening phase.

The Temptation to Skip Straight to Declaration

I need to be honest with you about something I see happening in many people's spiritual journey (including my own for many years):

We want the freedom without the listening.

We want to declare "I am who God says I am!" without actually doing the hard work of:

Sitting with our doubts

Acknowledging our wounds

Distinguishing God's voice from pain's voice

Bringing our messy reality to God

We want the declaration without the discovery. The breakthrough without the process. The truth that sets us free without the honest listening that makes truth real.

But it doesn't work that way.

Jesus said, "You will KNOW the truth, and the truth will set you free" (John 8:32). Not "You will recite the truth" or "You will perform the truth" or "You will declare the truth louder than your doubts."

You will KNOW it. And knowing comes through the kind of listening we've been practicing all week.

From Listening to Living: The Integration

Here's how the listening practices from this week change your daily life:

Day 1's Practice (Recognizing God has always been speaking):

Changes how you approach uncertainty: Instead of panic, you pause and ask, "What has God already spoken that I need to remember?"

Day 2's Practice (Distinguishing voices):

Changes how you respond to criticism: Instead of immediately believing negative words, you ask, "Whose voice is this? Does this sound like my Father?"

Day 3's Practice (Honest self-listening):

Changes how you handle emotions: Instead of numbing or managing, you bring them to God and ask, "What are You wanting to show me through this feeling?"

Day 4's Practice ("Tell me more" in relationships):

Changes how you connect with others: Instead of controlling conversations, you create space for authentic connection—which trains you to do the same with God

Day 5's Practice (Acknowledging the gap):

Changes how you approach spiritual growth: Instead of performing faith you don't feel, you bring God your honest struggles and let Him meet you there

All of these listening practices are preparing you to LIVE differently—not just believe differently.

What This Week Has Actually Been About

This week wasn't primarily about learning new information about your identity. It was about **developing the spiritual muscle of listening** so that when God speaks truth over you, you can actually recognize and receive it.

Think about it:

God has always been saying you're chosen (Day 1)

God's voice has always been calling you His child (Day 2)

God has always seen you as royal (Day 3)

The Spirit has always been testifying to your belonging (Day 4)

God has always loved you before the foundation of the world (Day 5)

The truths haven't changed. What's changing is your ability to HEAR them.

And that's what Week 1 has been building—your capacity to recognize God's voice speaking identity over you, above every other voice trying to define you.

The Next Step: From Hearing to Doing

James 1:22 warns us: "Be ye doers of the word, and not hearers only, deceiving yourselves."

So here's today's question: **What does it look like to "do" the listening you've been practicing?**

It means:

When anxiety rises, you pause and practice the "Whose voice is this?" question

When someone hurts you, you use "Tell me more" instead of immediately defending

When you feel unworthy, you bring that feeling to God instead of numbing it

When you're tempted to perform, you remember whose you are instead of proving who you are

Listening becomes living when the practices become reflexes.

Guided Questions for Reflection

Of the five days of listening practices this week, which one felt most uncomfortable or challenging? Why?

....

....

Where in your daily life this week did you actually USE one of the listening practices? What happened?

....

....

What specific situation are you facing right now where you need to apply listening before declaring?

(Example: a conflict where you need to listen to the other person's heart, a fear where you need to listen to what God is saying, etc.)

....

....

Complete this sentence: "This week's listening practices revealed that I've been __________ instead of actually hearing God's voice about my identity."

....

....

Bible Character Reflection

Gideon – When God called him "mighty warrior" (Judges 6:12), Gideon's immediate response wasn't declaration—it was doubt: "If the Lord is with us, why has all this happened?" (v.13)

Notice what God did: He didn't argue with Gideon's feelings. He didn't demand Gideon immediately "claim his identity." Instead, God **kept speaking, kept showing up, kept inviting Gideon into conversation** until the truth became real enough to act on.

Gideon needed time to LISTEN to God's voice calling him "mighty warrior" before he could LIVE like one. The listening came first. The living followed.

That's what this week has been—building your listening capacity so God's truth about you can actually take root.

Spiritual Practice: The Weekly Integration (20 minutes)

Part 1: Review Your Week (10 minutes)

Look back at your journal entries from Days 1-5. For each day, write one sentence:

Day 1: What did I learn about how God has been speaking?

Day 2: What did I learn about recognizing His voice?

Day 3: What did I learn about listening to myself honestly?

Day 4: What did I learn about listening in relationships?

Day 5: What did I learn about the gap between knowing and feeling?

Part 2: One Commitment (5 minutes)

Choose ONE listening practice from this week that you will continue daily next week. Write it as a specific commitment:

"This week I learned _________. Next week I will practice this by _________."

Part 3: Invitation to God (5 minutes)

Pray: *"Father, this week I've been learning to recognize Your voice. Show me one specific way this listening should change how I live this coming week."*

Then wait. Write what comes.

Prayer

Lord, thank You for this week of learning to listen. Thank You for being patient with my doubt, my struggle, my honest mess. I don't want to just hear truth—I want to KNOW it so deeply that it sets me free. Help me carry these listening practices into my daily life. When I'm tempted to skip straight to declaring truth I don't yet feel, remind me that listening comes first. Teach me to live from what I'm learning to hear. In Jesus' name, amen.

Daily Declaration

I am learning to listen before I declare.
I am learning to hear before I perform.
This week has prepared me to receive
the truth that will set me free.

Connection to Chapter 1 & Looking Ahead

This week completed Chapter 1's foundation: **"The journey of identity is not about constructing something new—it's about uncovering what's already there."** Through listening, you're uncovering God's voice that's been speaking all along.

Tomorrow (Day 7) we'll take a sacred pause to reflect on the entire week.

Then Week 2 will build on this foundation by exploring how your body, soul, and spirit work together in this identity journey—but only after you've developed the listening skills to hear what each part is communicating.

Quote of the Day

"You silence the lies not by shouting truth louder, but by learning to recognize whose voice is speaking. This week, you've been training your spiritual ears."

Day 7 – A Sacred Pause: Reflecting on the Voice That Defines You

Who God Says I Am

Scripture

"Be still, and know that I am God."
—Psalm 46:10 (KJV)

"The Lord will fight for you, and you have only to be silent."
—Exodus 14:14 (ESV)

Reflection

Welcome to Day 7—your sacred pause.

This isn't just another devotional to check off your list. This is the moment where you step back from doing and simply **be**—reflecting on what God has been speaking to you all week.

Chapter 1 of *Who Am Eye?* teaches us that transformation doesn't come from constant striving—it comes from learning to listen. This week, you've been practicing that listening. Today, we honor that work by creating space to hear what the Holy Spirit wants to highlight from these seven days.

I remember when I first learned the power of the sacred pause. I was in the middle of losing everything—my business, my reputation, my sense of self. I kept asking God, "What do I do next? What's the answer? How do I fix this?"

And in the silence, I finally heard Him whisper: **"Stop doing. Start being. You are not defined by what you accomplish—you're defined by whose you are."**

That pause changed everything. Not because I got immediate answers, but because I finally created space to **hear the voice that had been speaking all along**.

What This Week Has Been Building

Let's trace the journey you've been on:

Day 1: You learned that God has been speaking your name since before you were born. The question isn't whether He's speaking—it's whether you're listening.

Day 2: You practiced distinguishing God's voice from the competing voices of pain, performance, and people's opinions. You learned that the Father's voice sounds like love, even in correction.

Day 3: You discovered that listening to yourself honestly (your Actual Self) creates the space where God can speak truth. You can't proclaim you're chosen while refusing to acknowledge the voice inside that feels ordinary.

Day 4: You practiced listening in relationships, learning that how you listen to others trains you to hear God. The "Tell me more" prayer became a gateway to deeper connection.

Day 5: You brought God the gap between knowing truth and feeling it—learning that emotional honesty is the pathway to experiencing God's comfort, not an obstacle to faith.

Day 6: You explored how listening changes how you live—recognizing that hearing must come before declaring, and practices must become reflexes.

Today: You pause to let it all settle. To listen for what the Holy Spirit wants you to carry forward.

The Discipline of Stillness

Psalm 46:10 commands: "Be still, and know that I am God."

Notice the order: **Stillness comes before knowing.**

We live in a culture that values constant motion, immediate answers, and quick fixes. Even in our spiritual lives, we're tempted to rush from one truth to the next without letting it take root.

But God invites you to something different: **the sacred discipline of pausing long enough to let Him speak into what you've been learning.**

This is what Chapter 11 calls "A Sacred Pause—Reflecting on Your Journey Through God's Eyes." Before you move forward, you must look back and ask: "What has God been showing me about whose I am?"

Guided Questions for Weekly Reflection

Take your time with these questions. Don't rush. Let the Holy Spirit guide your reflection.

1. Looking back at Days 1-6, when did you most clearly hear God's voice speaking truth about who you are? What was He saying?

....

....

....

2. Which day's practice felt most uncomfortable or challenging? Why do you think that is?

....

....

....

3. What pattern did you notice about when you struggle to hear God's voice clearly?

(Examples: When you're anxious? When you're performing? When you're numbing emotions? When you're controlling conversations?)

....

....

....

4. Complete this sentence: "This week, I discovered that the biggest obstacle between me and hearing God's voice is..."

....

....

....

5. Which of your Four Selves showed up most this week?

False Self (reacting from wounds, needing control)

Presentable Self (managing image, performing spiritually)

Actual Self (honest about struggles and belovedness)

True Self (secure in God's love, listening from rest)

....

....

6. What one truth did God speak this week that you need to carry into Week 2?

....

....

....

Bible Character Reflection

Elijah – After his great victory over the prophets of Baal, Elijah ran in fear and exhaustion. He collapsed under a tree and asked God to take his life (1 Kings 19:4).

But notice what God did: He didn't give Elijah a pep talk or immediate answers. He gave him **rest, food, and silence** (v.5-8).

Then, after forty days, God invited Elijah to a cave where He would speak. A great wind came, then an earthquake, then fire—but **"the Lord was not in" any of these dramatic displays** (v.11-12).

Finally came "a still small voice" (v.12)—and **that** was where God spoke.

The lesson: Sometimes God's voice is clearest not in the dramatic moments, but in the sacred pause when you stop striving long enough to listen.

This week, you've been learning to recognize that still small voice above all the noise.

Spiritual Practice: The Weekly Sabbath Reflection (30-45 minutes)

Part 1: Gratitude Review (10 minutes)

Go back through your journal entries from Days 1-6. For each day, write one thing you're grateful God revealed to you.

Day 1: I'm grateful God showed me...

Day 2: I'm grateful I learned...

Day 3: I'm grateful I could be honest about...

Day 4: I'm grateful for the practice of...

Day 5: I'm grateful God met me when...

Day 6: I'm grateful this week changed how I...

Part 2: The Listening Prayer (15 minutes)

Find a quiet space. Sit comfortably. Close your eyes.

Pray: *"Holy Spirit, I've spent a week learning to listen. Now I'm creating space for You to speak. What do You most want me to know about what I've learned this week?"*

Then **be silent.** For at least 10 minutes. Don't fill the space. Don't perform. Just listen.

If thoughts come, write them down. If nothing comes, that's okay—the stillness itself is the practice.

Part 3: One Word Forward (5 minutes)

Ask God: *"If You could give me one word to carry into Week 2, what would it be?"*

Wait for a word to surface: Beloved. Chosen. Heard. Known. Rest. Trust. Listen. Freedom.

Write that word down. This is your theme for Week 2.

Part 4: Commit to Continue (5 minutes)

Review the listening practices from this week:

Distinguishing voices (Day 2)

Honest self-listening (Day 3)

"Tell me more" in relationships (Day 4)

Acknowledging the gap (Day 5)

Choose TWO practices you'll continue daily next week. Write them as commitments:

"This week I will continue practicing _________"

"This week I will continue practicing _________"

Prayer

Father, thank You for this week of learning to hear Your voice. Thank

You for every moment of stillness, every honest struggle, every time I heard You whisper my true name. As I pause today, I ask You to seal what You've been teaching me. Let it take deep root. Show me what You most want me to carry forward from this week. I'm listening, Father. Speak to Your child. In Jesus' name, amen.

Weekly Declaration

This week I learned that listening is the gateway to knowing.
I discovered that God's voice has been speaking all along—
I was just learning to recognize it above the noise.
Today I pause, I rest, I receive.
Tomorrow I continue the journey
of becoming who God says I am.

Looking Ahead to Week 2

Next week, we'll explore how your body, soul, and spirit work together in your identity formation. You'll discover:

How your body reveals which Self is leading

How your soul processes identity

How your spirit anchors you in whose you are

But all of that builds on this week's foundation: **learning to listen to the voice that defines you**.

Take today to rest in what God has spoken. Let the truth settle. Honor the sacred pause.

You are seen. You are loved. You are His.

This week, you learned to hear Him say it.

Quote of the Day

"Transformation doesn't happen in the noise of constant striving—it happens in the sacred pause when you finally stop long enough to hear whose you are."

Week 2: Body - Temple of the Holy Spirit (Chapter 2)

Day 8 – Your Body Tells the Truth About Which Self Is Leading

WHO GOD SAYS I AM

Scripture

"Or do you not know that your body is a temple of the Holy Spirit within you, whom you have from God? You are not your own, for you were bought with a price. So glorify God in your body."
—1 Corinthians 6:19-20 (ESV)

Reflection

Welcome to Week 2. Last week, you learned to **listen** to God's voice speaking your identity. This week, we're going to explore something you might not expect: **how your physical body reveals which voice you're actually following.**

Chapter 2 of *Who Am Eye?* teaches this profound truth: "Your body is not merely a shell for the soul and spirit, but a temple designed by God to house His presence."

But here's what I've discovered that changed everything: **Your body doesn't lie about which Self is leading your life.**

Let me explain what I mean.

When I'm living from my **True Self**—secure in God's love, resting in whose I am—my body reflects that. My shoulders relax. My breathing deepens. My presence with others is calm and genuine. I can sit in silence without needing to fill it. My physical state mirrors my spiritual security.

But when my **False Self** takes over—driven by wounds, fear, or the need to control—my body tells the truth before my mind catches up. Jaw clenched. Shoulders tight. Movements hurried and agitated. Even before I consciously realize I'm operating from fear, **my body is already broadcasting it.**

Your body is a truth-teller. It reveals which version of yourself is leading, often before you're aware of it.

How Your Body Reveals Your Four Selves

Chapter 2 teaches that depending on where you are spiritually and what life is throwing at you, different versions of yourself show up—**and your body expresses them physically:**

When Your True Self Is Leading:

Body language: Open, relaxed, genuinely present

Voice: Calm, steady, doesn't need to prove anything

Breathing: Deep, natural rhythm

Physical presence: People feel safe around you

You can be still without anxiety

When Your False Self Takes Over (wounded, reactive):

Body language: Defensive posture, crossed arms

Voice: Sharp, rushed, or withdrawn

Breathing: Shallow, holding breath

Physical presence: Others sense tension

Constant movement, can't settle

When Your Presentable Self Is Managing (image-focused):

Body language: Carefully controlled, performing

Voice: Modulated to say what others want to hear

Breathing: Controlled, held in

Physical presence: People sense something's "off"

Exhausted from maintaining the performance

When Your Actual Self Is Honest (messy reality):

Body language: Authentic, not performing

Voice: Real, sometimes shaky with emotion

Breathing: May be uneven but genuine

Physical presence: Vulnerable, human

Able to acknowledge physical needs

Your Body as Temple vs. Your Body as Tool

Last week you learned to listen to God's voice. This week, we're asking: **How does your body respond to that voice?**

Chapter 2 distinguishes between two ways we can relate to our bodies:

Living FOR your body (trying to make it perfect, acceptable, impressive) leads to:

Exhaustion from constant management

Shame when it doesn't measure up

Using your physical presence to earn approval

Living FROM your body as God's temple (surrendered, honored, used for His glory) leads to:

Rest in how He designed you

Gratitude for His presence within you

Your physical presence becoming an expression of His love

Guided Questions for Reflection

Right now, in this moment, what is your body telling you about which Self is leading?

(Check: Are your shoulders tense? Jaw clenched? Breathing shallow? Or relaxed, open, at peace?)

....

....

When you think about the truth that your body is God's temple, how does that change how you view your physical self?

....

....

In what specific situations does your body reveal that your False Self or Presentable Self has taken over?

(Examples: body tenses in conflict, voice changes when seeking approval, can't sit still when anxious)

....

....

What would it look like to honor your body as God's temple today—not by making it perfect, but by surrendering it to His purposes?

....

....

Bible Character Reflection

Jesus – Notice how often the Gospels record Jesus' physical actions: He touched lepers (Matthew 8:3). He wept at Lazarus' tomb (John 11:35). He overturned tables in righteous anger (Matthew 21:12). He grew weary and slept (Matthew 8:24). He felt compassion in His gut (Matthew 9:36—the Greek word literally means "moved in the bowels").

Jesus never separated His physical body from His spiritual mission. His body was the instrument through which divine love touched human need.

Like Jesus, your body is meant to be an instrument of God's presence in the world—not something to manage for approval, but something to surrender for His glory.

Spiritual Practice: Body Awareness Prayer (10 minutes)

Part 1: Physical Inventory (3 minutes)

Sit comfortably. Take three deep breaths. Now do a body scan:

Where is tension held? (Jaw? Shoulders? Stomach?)

What is your breathing like? (Shallow? Deep? Held?)

What is your posture communicating? (Defensive? Open? Tired?)

Don't judge it—just notice.

Part 2: Ask the Truth Question (3 minutes)

Now ask: *"Holy Spirit, what is my body trying to tell me right now about which Self has been leading?"*

Listen. If anxiety is in your chest, it might be False Self trying to control. If exhaustion is everywhere, it might be Presentable Self performing. If there's peace, it might be True Self resting in whose you are.

Part 3: Surrendered Offering (4 minutes)

Place your hands over your heart and pray:

"Father, this body is Your temple. I surrender it to You—not as a perfect offering, but as a living one. Thank You that You hold every cell together with cross-shaped proteins. Help me honor this temple today, not by making it impressive, but by letting it express Your presence. Where there's tension, bring Your peace. Where there's exhaustion, bring Your rest. I am Yours, body and spirit. Amen."

Prayer

Father, thank You for designing my body with such care. Thank You that You hold me together—literally—through Your power. Forgive me for the times I've treated my body as something to manage for approval rather than honor as Your temple. Today, help me notice what my body is telling me about which Self is leading. When I feel my shoulders tense or my breathing shallow, remind me to pause and ask: 'Whose voice am I following right now?' Let my physical presence reflect the peace of knowing I belong to You. In Jesus' name, amen.

Daily Declaration

My body is God's temple—
not a project to perfect, but a dwelling place to honor.
Today I pay attention to what my body reveals
about which Self is leading my life.

Connection to Week 1

Last week you learned to **listen** to God's voice above all others. This week you're learning that **your body reveals which voice you're actually following.**

When God's voice of love and security leads, your body responds with peace. When fear's voice leads, your body responds with tension. **Your physical state is the evidence of whose voice has the final word.**

Tomorrow, we'll explore how your soul processes the messages your body is revealing.

You are seen. You are loved. You are His.

And your body—held together by cross-shaped proteins—
proclaims that truth in every cell.

Quote of the Day

"Your body doesn't lie. It tells you which Self is leading before your mind catches up. Pay attention."

Day 9 – Held Together by the Cross

Who God Says I Am

Scripture

"For by him all things were created, in heaven and on earth, visible and invisible, whether thrones or dominions or rulers or authorities—all things were created through him and for him. And he is before all things, and in him all things hold together."
—Colossians 1:16-17 (ESV)

Reflection

Yesterday you discovered that your body is God's temple and that it reveals which Self is leading your life. Today, we go deeper into something that will absolutely astound you about God's intimate design.

There's a protein in your body called laminin. You've probably never heard of it, but it's one of the most important proteins in your entire physical system. Laminin is what holds your cells together. It's literally the glue that keeps your body from falling apart.

Here's what makes this extraordinary: When scientists look at laminin under a microscope, they discover that this essential protein—found in every living creature—naturally forms the shape of a cross.

Let that sink in for a moment.

The very thing holding every single cell in your body together is shaped like the cross on which Jesus died for you.

Colossians 1:17 says, "in him all things hold together." I used to read that as poetic language—a beautiful theological metaphor. But when I learned about laminin, I realized it's not just metaphor. It's biological reality.

Jesus Christ is not only upholding the universe by the word of His power (Hebrews 1:3), but He's holding every single cell in your body together through proteins shaped like the very cross on which He died for you.

The Personal Impact

When I first learned about laminin, I was in the middle of a season where I felt like I was falling apart. My ministry was struggling. My relationships were strained. My sense of self was fragmented.

I remember sitting in my office, looking at an image of laminin on my computer screen, and I wept.

Not because everything suddenly got better. But because I realized something profound: **Even when I feel like I'm falling apart, Christ is literally holding me together at the cellular level.**

Every breath I take. Every heartbeat. Every movement. Every moment of my existence is sustained by millions of tiny crosses working within me.

This isn't just theological truth—it's biological fact. **You are fearfully and wonderfully made, held together by His love in the most personal, distinctive, and miraculous way imaginable.**

What This Means for Your Identity

When you understand that Christ is holding you together—literally—it changes how you view your physical body:

Your body is not a random collection of cells. It's a masterpiece designed by God, held together by His power, displaying His glory at the molecular level.

Your physical struggles don't negate your worth. Whether you're dealing with chronic illness, physical limitations, or simply the wear of aging, Christ is still holding every cell together with cross-shaped love.

Your body was designed for worship. Not just in raising hands during a song, but in how you move through the world, how you care for this temple, how your physical presence becomes an expression of the

One who holds you together.

Guided Questions for Reflection

How does knowing that cross-shaped proteins hold your cells together change how you view your physical body?

....

....

....

In what areas of life do you currently feel like you're "falling apart"? How does Colossians 1:17 speak to that feeling?

....

....

....

What would it look like to honor your body today—not because it's perfect, but because Christ Himself holds it together?

....

....

....

How might remembering laminin's cross shape affect how you respond when your body experiences pain, limitation, or weakness?

....

....

....

My Thoughts

(Use this space to write any additional personal reflections about today's devotional)

....

....

....

....

Bible Character Reflection

Paul – He experienced physical affliction that he called a "thorn in the flesh" (2 Corinthians 12:7). Three times he begged God to remove it. But God's response wasn't healing—it was a deeper revelation: "My grace is sufficient for you, for my power is made perfect in weakness" (v.9).

Paul's body was held together by the same cross-shaped proteins that hold yours. His physical limitation didn't disqualify him from God's purpose—it became the very place where God's power was most clearly displayed.

Like Paul, your physical reality—whatever it is—doesn't diminish God's power working in you. Christ holds you together, thorns and all.

Spiritual Practice of the Day

The Laminin Meditation (10 minutes)

Find a quiet space. Sit or lie comfortably.

Part 1: Physical Awareness (3 minutes)

Place your hand over your heart and feel it beating

Take slow, deep breaths and notice your lungs expanding

Wiggle your fingers and toes, feeling the movement

Part 2: Meditation on Being Held (5 minutes)

As you breathe, repeat this truth silently:

Inhale: "Christ holds me together"

Exhale: "At every cellular level"

Visualize: Millions of tiny cross-shaped proteins throughout your entire body, holding every cell in place through Christ's power.

Part 3: Gratitude Prayer (2 minutes)

Pray aloud or silently:

"Jesus, thank You for not just holding the universe together—You're holding ME together. Every cell. Every breath. Every moment. When I feel like I'm falling apart, remind me of laminin—the cross-shaped protein proving that You've got me. My body is Yours. Hold me together today. Amen."

Prayer

Father, I am in awe. You didn't just create my body and walk away—You actively hold every single cell together through Your Son. When I look at laminin's cross shape, I see Your signature written into my very biology. Forgive me for taking this temple for granted. Forgive me for treating my body as something to manage for approval rather than honor as Your dwelling place. Today, help me remember: I am held together by the cross. Not metaphorically. Literally. And if You're holding me together at the cellular level, I can trust You with everything else that feels like it's falling apart. In Jesus' name, amen.

Daily Declaration

Christ holds me together—
not just spiritually, but physically.
Every cell in my body proclaims:
I am designed, sustained, and held by the cross.

You are seen. You are loved. You are His.
And every molecule of your being proves it.

Quote of the Day

"You are not held together by willpower or positive thinking. You are held together by cross-shaped love at the cellular level."

Day 10 – When Your Body Becomes a Weapon Instead of a Temple

Who God Says I Am

Scripture

"For we do not wrestle against flesh and blood, but against the rulers, against the authorities, against the cosmic powers over this present darkness, against the spiritual forces of evil in the heavenly places."
—Ephesians 6:12 (ESV)

"Do you not know that your bodies are members of Christ?"
—1 Corinthians 6:15 (ESV)

Reflection

Yesterday you discovered the wonder of laminin—how Christ holds your body together at the cellular level. Today we must address a harder truth: **Satan knows how precious your body is to God, and he works tirelessly to corrupt, distort, or defile your relationship with your physical being.**

This isn't comfortable to discuss, but it's essential for reclaiming your identity.

Chapter 2 of *Who Am Eye?* teaches: "The body forms such a crucial part of our human identity, and the enemy is fully aware of this. If he can manage to destroy, distort, or defile our relationship with our physical being, he has won a significant part of the identity battle."

Think about it: How did Satan tempt Eve? Through her physical senses—what she saw, heard, and desired to taste (Genesis 3:6). He used her God-given physical design against her, leading her into deception through sensory stimulation.

This same strategy continues today.

When Your Body Becomes a Battlefield

I need to be honest with you about my own struggle. For years, I used my body as a weapon—not against others, but against myself.

When ministry stress intensified, I would:

Push through exhaustion instead of resting

Skip meals or overeat to numb emotions

Ignore my body's signals that I needed help

Use physical busyness to avoid dealing with soul issues

I told myself I was "sacrificing for the kingdom." But what I was actually doing was **treating God's temple with contempt while calling it devotion.**

My body wasn't functioning as a temple for worship—it had become a battlefield where I fought against my own limitations, punished myself for not being enough, and tried to prove my worth through relentless performance.

That's not what God designed your body for.

The Enemy's Three Primary Attacks on Your Body

Based on Chapter 2's teaching, here are the main ways Satan targets your physical identity:

1. Body Image Distortion

Making you hate what God designed

Obsessing over appearance instead of stewardship

Comparing your temple to others' temples

Finding worth in physical attractiveness rather than divine inhabitation

2. Physical Abuse/Neglect

Overwork that destroys health

Addictions that defile the temple

Self-harm in any form

Refusing rest, food, or basic care

3. Sexual Immorality

Using the body for purposes God never intended

Joining Christ's body to sin (1 Corinthians 6:15-16)

Treating sexuality as casual rather than sacred

If the enemy can convince you that your body is yours to do with as you please, he's already won a major battle.

The Truth That Sets You Free

Here's the liberating counter-truth from 1 Corinthians 6:19-20:

"You are not your own, for you were bought with a price. So glorify God in your body."

You don't own your body. Christ bought it. It's His temple now.

This isn't restriction—this is **freedom**. When you understand that your body belongs to God:

You're free from the tyranny of having to make it perfect

You're free from shame when it's weak or limited

You're free from using it to earn approval

You're free to steward it for His glory, not your image

Reclaiming Your Body as Sacred Space

The enemy wants your body to be:

A source of shame

A tool for proving worth

A weapon against yourself or others

A temple to lesser gods (success, appearance, pleasure)

But God says your body is:

His dwelling place

An instrument of righteousness

A temple for worship

A vessel for His glory

The battle for your identity is being fought on physical ground. Which voice will you let define how you treat this temple?

Guided Questions for Reflection

In what ways have you been treating your body as a weapon (against yourself or others) rather than a temple?

....

....

....

Which of the three enemy attacks (body image distortion, physical abuse/neglect, sexual immorality) do you most struggle with? Be specific.

....

....

....

Complete this sentence: "I have been using my body to ________ instead of glorifying God."

....

....

What would change if you truly believed your body is not yours, but Christ's temple that He bought with His blood?

....

....

....

My Thoughts

(Use this space to write any additional personal reflections about today's devotional)

....

....

....

....

Bible Character Reflection

Daniel – When taken captive to Babylon, one of the first battles Daniel faced was over his body. The king offered royal food and wine, but Daniel "resolved that he would not defile himself" (Daniel 1:8).

This wasn't about dietary preference—it was about **whose temple his body was.** In a foreign land where everything was being taken from him,

Daniel's body remained sacred ground that belonged to God alone.

The result? God gave Daniel and his friends better health, greater wisdom, and divine favor (v.15-20). When you honor your body as God's temple, He honors that stewardship.

Like Daniel, you're living in a culture that constantly offers you ways to defile the temple. Your body is sacred ground. Guard it accordingly.

Spiritual Practice of the Day

The Reclamation Prayer (15 minutes)

Part 1: Confession (5 minutes)

Be brutally honest with God about how you've been treating His temple. Write or pray aloud:

"Father, I confess that I have treated my body as _________ instead of Your temple. I have used it to _________. I have neglected it by _________. I have defiled it through _________."

Don't hold back. He already knows. Confession brings it into the light.

Part 2: Renunciation (5 minutes)

Now renounce the enemy's lies and attacks:

"In Jesus' name, I renounce the lie that my body is mine to do with as I please. I renounce using my body as a weapon. I renounce [specific attack you identified]. I break agreement with every way I've treated this temple with contempt."

Part 3: Reclamation (5 minutes)

Now surrender your body back to its rightful Owner:

"Father, I surrender this body back to You. It's not mine—it's Yours. You bought it with Jesus' blood. You hold it together with cross-shaped proteins. Today I reclaim this temple for Your glory. Use my hands for Your work. Use my mouth for Your words. Use my physical presence for Your purposes. This body is Yours. Amen."

Prayer

Lord Jesus, forgive me for treating Your temple carelessly. Forgive me for using my body as a weapon when You designed it as a sanctuary. I see now how the enemy has been attacking my physical identity, trying to make me hate what You created, abuse what You're sustaining, or defile what You've made holy. Today I take back this ground. My body is not mine—it's Yours. Bought with Your blood. Held together by Your power. Indwelt by Your Spirit. Help me honor this temple, not through perfectionism, but through grateful stewardship. When the enemy whispers lies about my body, remind me: This is sacred ground. In Your name, amen.

Daily Declaration

My body is not a weapon—it's a temple.
It's not mine to abuse—it belongs to Christ.
Today I reclaim this sacred ground
and surrender it to its rightful Owner.

You are seen. You are loved. You are His.
And your body is holy ground.

Quote of the Day

"The enemy wants you to hate your body or worship it. God wants you to honor it as the temple it was designed to be."

Day 11 – Your Physical Presence as Ministry

Who God Says I Am

Scripture

"So, whether you eat or drink, or whatever you do, do all to the glory of God."
—1 Corinthians 10:31 (ESV)

"Go therefore and make disciples of all nations, baptizing them in the name of the Father and of the Son and of the Holy Spirit, teaching them to observe all that I have commanded you."
—Matthew 28:19-20 (ESV)

Reflection

For the past three days, you've been learning that your body is God's temple—held together by cross-shaped proteins, designed for His glory, and meant to be reclaimed from the enemy's attacks.

Today we shift from defense to offense: **Your physical form wasn't created merely for survival or personal pleasure—it was designed for worship AND service.**

Chapter 2 of *Who Am Eye?* teaches: "Your hands become His hands to heal and comfort. Your feet become His feet to carry the good news. Your voice becomes His voice to speak truth and encouragement. Your very presence becomes a tangible expression of His love in this world."

This hit me powerfully several years ago during a mission trip. I was visiting a rural village where I would be preaching. Before the service, a young mother brought her sick child to me—not because I'm a doctor, but because I represented Christ's physical presence in their community.

As I held that child and prayed, something profound struck me: My arms were Christ's arms holding this child. My voice was speaking His comfort. My physical presence was ministry.

The Incarnational Truth

Jesus didn't redeem humanity from a distance. He took on flesh. He touched lepers. He wept at graves. He broke bread with sinners. He let His physical body be broken for us.

The Incarnation teaches us that physical presence matters to God.

When you visit someone in the hospital, your body is ministry.
When you hug someone who's grieving, your body is ministry.
When you sit in silence with someone suffering, your body is ministry.
When you use your hands to serve, your body is ministry.

Your physical form is not separate from your spiritual calling—it's the instrument through which that calling is fulfilled.

From Self-Consciousness to Service

Here's what I've discovered about the Four Selves and physical ministry:

False Self uses the body for self-protection—keeping distance, avoiding touch, staying "safe" from others' pain.

Presentable Self uses the body for image management—making sure we look spiritual, capable, together.

Actual Self brings our physical limitations honestly—acknowledging when we're tired, hurting, or overwhelmed, while still showing up.

True Self surrenders the body as an instrument of God's love—not perfect, not impressive, just available.

The shift from self-consciousness to service happens when you stop asking "How do I look?" and start asking "How can I serve?"

Your Commission Requires Your Body

Matthew 28:19-20 doesn't say "spiritually contemplate making disciples." It says **GO.** That requires feet. It says **baptize.** That requires hands. It says **teach.** That requires a voice.

The Great Commission is a physical assignment that requires your physical presence.

Where has God placed your body right now?

In a workplace where people need to see Christ's love demonstrated?

In a family where your physical presence provides stability?

In a community where your hands can serve practical needs?

In a church where your voice can speak encouragement?

Your body is exactly where God wants it to be for ministry today.

Guided Questions for Reflection

How has viewing your body primarily as something to manage for appearance kept you from using it for ministry?

....

....

....

Where has God placed your physical body right now, and who needs Christ's tangible presence through you?

....

....

....

What would change if you woke up each morning and asked: "Father, how do You want to use my hands, feet, voice, and presence for Your glory today?"

....

....

....

Which Self typically shows up when you're called to physical ministry—False (self-protective), Presentable (image-managing), Actual (honest about limitations), or True (surrendered for service)?

....

....

....

My Thoughts

(Use this space to write any additional personal reflections about today's devotional)

....

....

....

....

Bible Character Reflection

Jesus – Every healing in the Gospels involved His physical presence and touch:

He touched the leper (Matthew 8:3)

He took the little girl's hand (Mark 5:41)

He put His fingers in the deaf man's ears (Mark 7:33)

He made mud and anointed the blind man's eyes (John 9:6)

Jesus could have healed from a distance—He did on occasion. But most often, **He chose to show up physically.** His body was the primary instrument of His earthly ministry.

Like Jesus, your physical presence is not incidental to your ministry—it IS your ministry in many situations.

Spiritual Practice of the Day

The Morning Offering of the Body (5 minutes)

Tomorrow morning (or right now if it's morning), before checking your phone or starting your day, practice this:

Part 1: Physical Positioning (1 minute)

Stand with your feet shoulder-width apart. Extend your arms out to your sides (forming a cross with your body). Close your eyes.

Part 2: The Offering Prayer (3 minutes)

Pray aloud, touching each body part as you offer it:

"Father, today I offer You my temple:

My feet (touch your feet)—send me where You want me to go

My hands (extend your hands)—use them to serve as You would serve

My mouth (touch your lips)—let my words be Yours

My eyes (touch your eyes)—help me see people as You see them

My ears (touch your ears)—let me hear the needs You want me to meet

My heart (place hand over heart)—fill it with Your compassion

My whole body—this temple is Yours for service today

Not my will, but Yours. Not my agenda, but Yours. Use me. Amen."

Part 3: One Specific Commitment (1 minute)

Ask: "Holy Spirit, show me ONE specific way You want me to use my physical presence for ministry today."

Wait. Listen. Then do it.

Prayer

Father, forgive me for the times I've been so focused on how my body looks that I've forgotten what it's for. You didn't give me this temple to admire in the mirror—You gave it to me to carry Your presence into the world. Today, I surrender my physical form to You—not as a perfect offering, but as a living one. Use my hands to comfort. Use my feet to go where people are hurting. Use my voice to speak Your truth. Use my very presence to remind someone that they're not alone. I'm not asking You to make me impressive—I'm asking You to make me available. In Jesus' name, amen.

Daily Declaration

My body is not for display—it's for deployment.
Today I surrender my physical presence
as an instrument of God's love in the world.

You are seen. You are loved. You are His.
And your presence matters more than you know.

Quote of the Day

"The world doesn't need more people who look spiritual. It needs people whose bodies show up where love is needed."

Day 12 – The Body's Hunger for Rest

Who God Says I Am

Scripture

"Come to me, all who labor and are heavy laden, and I will give you rest. Take my yoke upon you, and learn from me, for I am gentle and lowly in heart, and you will find rest for your souls."
—Matthew 11:28-29 (ESV)

"It is in vain that you rise up early and go late to rest, eating the bread of anxious toil; for he gives to his beloved sleep."
—Psalm 127:2 (ESV)

Reflection

Yesterday you learned that your body is designed for service and ministry. Today we must balance that truth with something equally important: **Your body is also designed for rest.**

This is where many of us—especially those in ministry or driven by performance—get it dangerously wrong.

Chapter 2 of *Who Am Eye?* addresses this directly: "I had been treating my body like an obstacle to spiritual growth, pushing through exhaustion, ignoring stress signals, believing that somehow denying my physical needs made me more spiritual. In those seasons when my body was exhausted, my soul felt depleted, even though I was working for the Lord."

I wrote those words from painful experience. For years, I equated spiritual maturity with physical tirelessness. If I was tired, I prayed for more strength. If I was hungry, I fasted. If I needed rest, I pushed through.

I told myself I was "sacrificing for the kingdom." But what I was actually doing was **treating God's temple with contempt while calling it devotion.**

The Lie of Relentless Productivity

Our culture—and sadly, even church culture—often glorifies exhaustion:

"I'll sleep when I'm dead"

"No days off when you're building the kingdom"

"Rest is for the weak"

"Hustle harder"

But here's the truth that set me free: **God gives His beloved sleep (Psalm 127:2). If He wanted you to be perpetually productive, He wouldn't have designed your body to require rest.**

Jesus slept. Even in a storm (Matthew 8:24). He withdrew to lonely places to rest (Luke 5:16). He sat by a well while His disciples went for food (John 4:6). He modeled the rhythm of work and rest.

If Jesus needed rest, what makes us think we don't?

When Rest Becomes Resistance

Here's what I've learned about rest and the Four Selves:

False Self views rest as weakness and pushes through exhaustion to prove worth.

Presentable Self can't rest because rest might reveal limitations or cause others to think less of us.

Actual Self can acknowledge: "I'm tired. I need rest. That's okay."

True Self rests as an act of worship—trusting that God holds everything together even when we stop working.

Your Body's Warning System

God designed your body with built-in signals that you need rest:

Fatigue

Irritability

Difficulty concentrating

Physical tension

Emotional reactivity

Weakened immune system

These aren't failures to overcome—they're messages from the temple that it needs maintenance.

When you ignore these signals, you're not being spiritual—you're being foolish. And eventually, your body will force you to rest through illness, injury, or complete burnout.

I know this because it happened to me. My body shut down when I wouldn't listen. The rest I refused to take willingly, I eventually took unwillingly.

The Sabbath Principle

God didn't suggest rest—He commanded it. The fourth commandment isn't "Remember the Sabbath day, unless you're really busy." It's a non-negotiable principle woven into creation itself.

Even God rested on the seventh day (Genesis 2:2-3)—not because He was tired, but to establish a pattern for His image-bearers.

Rest isn't laziness. Rest is obedience.

Rest isn't unproductive. Rest is worship.

Rest isn't selfish. Rest is stewardship of the temple God gave you.

Guided Questions for Reflection

What lies have you believed about rest that keep you from honoring your body's need for it?

....

....

....

Which Self typically resists rest in your life—False (proving worth through productivity) or Presentable (maintaining an image of tirelessness)?

....

....

....

What warning signals is your body currently giving you that

you've been ignoring?

....

....

....

Complete this sentence: "If I truly believed God gives His beloved sleep, I would change _________."

....

....

....

My Thoughts

(Use this space to write any additional personal reflections about today's devotional)

....

....

....

....

Bible Character Reflection

Elijah – After his great victory over the prophets of Baal, Elijah ran in exhaustion and collapsed under a tree, asking God to take his life (1 Kings 19:4).

Notice God's response: He didn't rebuke Elijah for being tired. He didn't preach at him about having more faith. **He gave him food and sleep** (v.5-6). Twice.

Then, after Elijah was physically restored, God addressed his spiritual and emotional state.

The lesson: Sometimes the most spiritual thing you can do is take a nap. God cares about your body's needs, and He's not impressed by your exhaustion.

Like Elijah, you may need physical rest before you can hear God clearly again.

Spiritual Practice of the Day

The Rest Audit (20 minutes)

Part 1: Honest Assessment (10 minutes)

Answer these questions honestly:

How many hours of sleep did you get last night? ___________

When was the last time you took a full day off from work/ministry? ___________

Do you regularly eat meals sitting down, or do you eat on the run? ___________

What physical activities bring you joy and renewal? ___________

When do you feel most rested? ___________

Part 2: Identify the Resistance (5 minutes)

Complete these sentences:

"I resist rest because ___________"

"If I rest, I'm afraid ___________"

"The voice that tells me rest is weakness sounds like ___________"

Part 3: One Change This Week (5 minutes)

Choose ONE specific way you will honor your body's need for rest this week:

Go to bed 30 minutes earlier

Take one full day off

Say no to one commitment

Take a 15-minute walk outside

Sit down for all meals

Schedule a nap

Write it here as a commitment: ___________

Prayer

Father, forgive me for treating rest as weakness when You designed it as worship. Forgive me for pushing my body beyond what You intended, calling it devotion when it was actually pride. Teach me the rhythm of work and rest that Jesus modeled. Help me trust that when I stop, You don't. When I sleep, You're still holding everything together. Give me the courage to rest—not because I've earned it, but because You commanded it and my body needs it. Let me honor this temple by giving it the rest required to serve You well. In Jesus' name, amen.

Daily Declaration

Rest is not laziness—it's obedience.

God gives His beloved sleep,
and today I receive that gift without guilt.

You are seen. You are loved. You are His.

Even when you're resting.

Quote of the Day

"Your body will force you to take the rest you refuse to schedule. Choose rest as worship before it becomes a forced shutdown."

Day 13 – Surrendering Your Temple Daily

WHO GOD SAYS I AM

Scripture

"I appeal to you therefore, brothers, by the mercies of God, to present your bodies as a living sacrifice, holy and acceptable to God, which is your spiritual worship."
—Romans 12:1 (ESV)

Reflection

We're nearing the end of Week 2, and it's time to bring together everything you've learned about your body as God's temple.

You've discovered that:

Christ holds your body together with cross-shaped proteins (Day 9)

Your body can become a weapon when the enemy attacks it (Day 10)

Your physical presence is ministry (Day 11)

Your body needs rest as an act of worship (Day 12)

Today, we address the daily practice that ties it all together: **surrendering your body as a living sacrifice.**

Romans 12:1 calls this "your spiritual worship"—not singing songs or raising hands, but the daily decision to say, "Father, this body is Yours. Use it for Your glory today."

What "Living Sacrifice" Actually Means

Here's the problem with being a living sacrifice: **living sacrifices keep trying to crawl off the altar.**

A dead sacrifice stays put. But when you present your body as a living sacrifice, you have to keep choosing surrender, day after day, moment after moment.

This is the daily battle I face—and you probably do too:

Will I use my body for God's purposes or my own agenda?

Will I honor this temple or treat it with contempt?

Will I rest when needed or push through exhaustion?

Will I let my physical presence serve others or protect myself?

Surrender isn't a one-time decision. It's a daily practice.

The Morning Offering

Chapter 2 teaches this crucial practice: "Every morning when you wake up—before you check your phone, before you worry about your schedule—you have the opportunity to surrender your eyes, your hands, your mouth, your heart to God's service."

I started doing this years ago, and it transformed not just my ministry, but my entire relationship with God.

When I consciously offer my body to Him each morning, I'm acknowledging that I am His chosen vessel, and everything I do with this physical form matters to Him.

Here's what this looks like practically:

Before my feet hit the floor, I pray: *"Father, this body is Yours today. My hands—use them for Your work. My feet—send me where You want me. My mouth—let it speak Your words. My eyes—help me see as You see. This temple is Yours. Fill it. Use it. Guide it. I surrender."*

This simple practice changes everything about how I move through my day.

Surrender in the Mundane

Here's what surprised me most about daily surrender: It's not just for "spiritual" activities.

When you surrender your body as a living sacrifice:

Washing dishes becomes an act of worship

Exercise becomes stewardship of the temple
Eating becomes communion with the Creator who sustains you
Sleep becomes trust that God holds everything when you rest
Work becomes using your hands as His hands

There's no longer a division between "sacred" and "secular" when your entire body has been surrendered to God.

When Surrender Feels Difficult

Some days, surrender feels natural. Other days, every part of you resists.

Your **False Self** wants to keep control, protect itself, prove its worth. Your **Presentable Self** wants to use your body to manage how others see you.

Your **Actual Self** can honestly admit: "I don't want to surrender today. I want to do what I want."

But your **True Self** knows the freedom that comes from daily surrender—the peace of not having to be in control, the joy of being used for something bigger than yourself.

The choice is always yours. And it's a choice you'll make again tomorrow, and the next day, and the day after that.

Guided Questions for Reflection

What would it look like to start every morning by surrendering your body to God before you do anything else?

....

....

....

In what specific area are you most resistant to surrendering your body to God's purposes?

(Examples: sleep schedule, eating habits, physical appearance, sexual purity, rest, service)

....

....

....

How might your daily activities (work, meals, exercise,

relationships) change if you truly viewed your body as a living sacrifice?

....

....

....

Complete this prayer: "Father, the hardest part of my body to surrender to You is _______ because _______."

....

....

....

My Thoughts

(Use this space to write any additional personal reflections about today's devotional)

....

....

....

....

Bible Character Reflection

Mary (Mother of Jesus) – When the angel Gabriel appeared to her with news that would change her life forever, Mary's response was simple but profound: "Behold, I am the servant of the Lord; let it be to me according to your word" (Luke 1:38).

She surrendered her body to be the vessel through which God would enter the world. She didn't know all the implications. She didn't have all the answers. **She simply said yes to God using her physical body for His purposes.**

Like Mary, your daily surrender doesn't require understanding everything God will do—just willingness to let Him use the temple He's given you.

Spiritual Practice of the Day

The Daily Surrender Ritual (Create Your Own)

Today, create a personal morning surrender ritual you'll commit to for the next week (and hopefully beyond).

Part 1: Choose Your Components (5 minutes)

Select 2-3 elements that resonate with you:

Physical positioning (standing, kneeling, hands open)

Speaking surrender over specific body parts

Scripture declaration (Romans 12:1, 1 Corinthians 6:19-20)

Silent meditation on being God's temple

Writing a short prayer of surrender

Part 2: Write Your Ritual (10 minutes)

Write out exactly what you'll do each morning. Be specific:

"Every morning before _______, I will _______ and pray _______."

Example: *"Every morning before checking my phone, I will stand with my hands open and pray: 'Father, this body is Yours. Use my hands, feet, mouth, and heart for Your glory today. I surrender this temple to You.'"*

Part 3: Commit and Test (5 minutes)

Practice your ritual right now. Then commit to doing it every morning for the next 7 days.

Set a reminder on your phone if needed. Put a note by your bed. Whatever it takes to establish this practice.

Prayer

Father, I am standing at the altar with this body—Your temple—and I'm making a choice. Not just once, but daily. This morning and every morning, I surrender this physical form to You. Not because it's perfect, but because it's Yours. You bought it with blood. You hold it together with cross-shaped love. You designed it for worship and service. Help me remember that when I wake up tomorrow and every day after. When my body wants to crawl off the altar and take back control, remind me: This is spiritual worship. This is what love looks like. This is freedom. I surrender. Again. In Jesus' name, amen.

Daily Declaration

Today I present my body as a living sacrifice—
not perfect, not impressive,
just surrendered to the One who made it,
bought it, and sustains it.

You are seen. You are loved. You are His.

Temple, altar, and offering—all in one.

Day 14 – Sacred Pause: What Is Your Body Revealing?

Who God Says I Am

Scripture

"Be still, and know that I am God."
—Psalm 46:10 (KJV)

"For you formed my inward parts; you knitted me together in my mother's womb. I praise you, for I am fearfully and wonderfully made."
—Psalm 139:13-14 (ESV)

Reflection

Welcome to Day 14—your second sacred pause.

This week, you've journeyed deep into understanding your body as God's temple. You've learned that Christ holds you together at the cellular level, that the enemy attacks your physical identity, that your presence is ministry, that rest is worship, and that daily surrender is spiritual service.

Today, we pause. We breathe. We reflect on what God has been revealing through your physical being.

Chapter 2 of *Who Am Eye?* teaches: "Your body tells the story of which version of yourself is leading. When you learn to pay attention to what your physical self is communicating, it becomes a powerful tool for recognizing when you need to realign with who God created you to be."

So today's question is simple but profound: **What is your body**

telling you right now about whose voice you're following?

The Body Scan Reflection

Before you answer any questions or read further, I want you to do something you've been practicing all week: **Listen to your body.**

Right now, in this moment:

Where is tension held? (Check your jaw, shoulders, stomach, hands)

What is your breathing like? (Shallow? Deep? Held?)

What is your posture communicating? (Closed? Open? Tired?)

What physical sensations are you aware of? (Pain? Comfort? Restlessness?)

Don't judge it. Don't try to fix it yet. Just notice.

Your body is telling you a story about which Self has been leading this week. Are you listening?

Weekly Integration Questions

Take your time with these. This is not a race. This is a sacred pause.

1. Looking back at Days 8-13, when did you most clearly sense that your body is God's temple? What shifted in that moment?

....

....

....

....

2. Which day's teaching felt most uncomfortable or challenging? Why do you think that particular truth triggered resistance?

....

....

....

3. The Laminin Discovery (Day 9): How has knowing about cross-shaped proteins changed how you view your physical body?

....

....

....

4. Enemy Attacks (Day 10): In what specific way has the enemy been targeting your relationship with your physical body? How will

you reclaim that ground?

....

....

....

5. Physical Presence as Ministry (Day 11): Where has God placed your body right now, and who needs Christ's tangible presence through you this week?

....

....

....

6. Rest as Worship (Day 12): What lie about rest did you identify, and what one change are you committing to make?

....

....

....

7. Daily Surrender (Day 13): Did you establish a morning surrender ritual? If yes, how did it change your day? If no, what stopped you?

....

....

....

8. Body Truth-Telling: What pattern did you notice this week about when your body reveals that False Self or Presentable Self is leading?

....

....

....

My Thoughts

(Use this space to write any additional personal reflections about Week 2)

....

....

....

....

....

....

The Integration Practice (30 minutes)

Part 1: Gratitude for Your Temple (10 minutes)

Write a letter to God, thanking Him for specific aspects of your body:

"Father, thank You for my_______ (hands, feet, eyes, etc.) that allow me to_______. Thank You that You hold me together with cross-shaped love. Thank You for designing this temple with such care..."

Be specific. Be grateful. Let this be worship.

Part 2: Body Confession and Reclamation (10 minutes)

Be honest about how you've been treating God's temple:

"Father, I confess that this week I _______. I have treated Your temple with_______. But today I reclaim this body as Yours. I surrender _______."

Part 3: Week 3 Preparation (10 minutes)

Next week, you'll explore your soul—the processing center where thoughts, emotions, and will intersect.

Ask God: *"Holy Spirit, what do I need to know about my soul as we begin Week 3? What are You preparing to reveal?"*

Wait. Listen. Write what comes.

Prayer

Father, thank You for this week of rediscovering what it means to have a body that is Yours. Thank You for laminin holding every cell together with cross-shaped love. Thank You for exposing the enemy's attacks on my physical identity. Thank You for teaching me that my presence matters, that rest is worship, and that daily surrender is spiritual service. As I pause today, show me what my body has been trying to tell me about which Self is leading my life. Help me honor this temple—not through perfectionism, but through grateful stewardship. Prepare my heart for Week 3 as I learn about my soul. I'm listening. In Jesus' name, amen.

Weekly Declaration

This week I learned that my body is not an obstacle—
it's a temple, held together by the cross,
designed for worship and service,
and honored through both work and rest.
I am fearfully and wonderfully made.

Looking Ahead to Week 3

Next week, you'll move from body to soul—the processing center where your intellect, will, and emotions work together (or sometimes against each other) to shape your identity.

You'll discover:

How your soul functions as mission control for your inner life

Why emotions are data, not directives

How trauma hijacks your soul's processing

The difference between soul healing and soul management

How your soul reveals which Self is leading

Take today to rest in what God has spoken about your body. Let the truth settle. Honor the sacred pause.

Tomorrow, we journey deeper.

You are seen. You are loved. You are His.

Body, soul, and spirit—all designed by Him, all belonging to Him.

Quote of the Day

"Your body doesn't lie about which Self is leading. This week, you learned to listen to what it's been trying to tell you."

Week 3: Soul - The Processing Center (Chapter 3)

Day 15 – Your Soul: Where Your Real Story Is Stored

Who God Says I Am

Scripture

"Why are you cast down, O my soul, and why are you in turmoil within me? Hope in God; for I shall again praise him, my salvation and my God."

—Psalm 42:5-6 (ESV)

"And the very God of peace sanctify you wholly; and I pray God your whole spirit and soul and body be preserved blameless unto the coming of our Lord Jesus Christ."

—1 Thessalonians 5:23 (KJV)

Reflection

Welcome to Week 3. For the past two weeks, you've been learning to listen to God's voice (Week 1) and understand your body as His temple (Week 2). Now we journey deeper—into the soul.

If the body is the house everyone sees from the street, **the soul is where you actually live**—behind closed doors, in the quiet moments, in the spaces between your public persona and your private reality.

Chapter 3 of *Who Am Eye?* teaches: "Now we get personal. Now we dive deep below the surface of what is visible to the naked eye. We're moving inward to the soul—that hidden, sacred space where your real story is stored."

This is where nobody else can see. Where you wrestle with your deepest questions. Where your strongest emotions live. And where your identity is truly forged.

What Is the Soul?

Think of your soul as **mission control for your inner life.** It's where three essential systems work together:

Intellect (Radar System) — gathering and processing information about who you are

Will (Flight Controller) — making decisions about what gets permission to "land" in your heart

Emotions (Weather System) — affecting how everything feels and flows

When your soul's control tower is functioning well—aligned with God's truth—you experience peace, clear thinking, and wise decisions. But when there's interference, storms, or poor communication between systems, chaos results.

And this is often when different versions of yourself take over.

The Soul's Hidden Wounds

Here's what I've discovered through my own journey: the soul is where we carry our deepest wounds. Not physical scars, but emotional and spiritual ones.

Chapter 3 explains: "At birth, our soul is pure—unstained by toxic relationships, trauma, or sin. But as life unfolds, we encounter experiences that leave deep impressions on the soul."

These experiences shape which versions of ourselves we learn to rely on:

When the soul is wounded, **False Self** develops protective strategies

When the soul fears exposure, **Presentable Self** carefully curates what's shown

When the soul is honest, **Actual Self** can acknowledge both brokenness and belovedness

When the soul is healed, **True Self** emerges more consistently

Your soul holds the story of how you got here—and that story shapes which Self shows up in different situations.

David's Soul Practice

Notice what David does repeatedly in the Psalms—he **talks to his soul:**

"Why are you cast down, O my soul?" (Psalm 42:5)
"Bless the Lord, O my soul" (Psalm 103:1)
"Return, O my soul, to your rest" (Psalm 116:7)

David didn't ignore his soul's condition. He didn't pretend everything was fine when it wasn't. He **acknowledged the turmoil, brought it before God, then redirected his hope.**

This is the practice we're developing this week: **listening to what's happening in your soul, bringing it honestly to God, and letting Him restore what's been damaged.**

Why This Week Matters

Many Christians focus on spirit (communion with God) and body (practical living), but neglect the soul—the processing center where transformation actually happens.

You can know all the right theology (intellect), but if your soul is processing life through unhealed wounds, you'll keep responding from False Self patterns.

You can make right decisions (will), but if your soul believes lies about your worth, those decisions won't stick.

You can manage your emotions (feelings), but if your soul hasn't brought them to God for healing, you're just performing control rather than experiencing peace.

This week is about soul care—not soul management.

Guided Questions for Reflection

When you think about your soul as "where your real story is stored," what story has your soul been telling about who you are?

....

....

....

Complete David's question for yourself: "Why are you cast down, O my soul?" What turmoil is your soul currently processing?

....

....

....

Of your three soul systems (intellect, will, emotions), which one tends to dominate? Which one gets neglected?

....

....

....

What would it look like to practice "soul honesty" with God this week—bringing Him the real condition of your inner life without performing spirituality?

....

....

....

My Thoughts

(Use this space to write any additional personal reflections about today's devotional)

....

....

....

....

Bible Character Reflection

David – Throughout the Psalms, David models radical soul honesty:

He admits depression: "My tears have been my food day and night" (Psalm 42:3)

He confesses rage: "Break their teeth, O God, in their mouth" (Psalm 58:6)

He expresses doubt: "How long, O Lord? Will you forget me forever?" (Psalm 13:1)

He celebrates joy: "You turned my mourning into dancing" (Psalm 30:11)

David didn't have a perfect soul—he had an honest one. He brought God the full range of his internal experience, and God called him "a man after my own heart" (1 Samuel 13:14).

Like David, your soul's honesty—not perfection—is what God desires.

Spiritual Practice of the Day

The Soul Conversation (15 minutes)

Part 1: Talk TO Your Soul (5 minutes)

Following David's example, speak directly to your soul. Write or say aloud:

"O my soul, what are you feeling right now? What are you afraid of? What are you hoping for? What lies have you been believing?"

Don't censor. Don't spiritualize yet. Just let your soul speak.

Part 2: Listen to Your Soul's Response (5 minutes)

Now be quiet and listen. What does your soul need to tell you? Write down what surfaces—thoughts, feelings, memories, fears, hopes.

Part 3: Bring It to God (5 minutes)

Now take everything your soul just revealed and bring it to your Heavenly Father:

"Father, this is the condition of my soul right now: _______. I'm not pretending. I'm not performing. This is the truth. Meet me here. Speak to my soul about who I really am."

Wait. Listen. Write what you hear.

Prayer

Father, thank You for creating me with a soul—a sacred inner space where my real story is stored. Thank You that You're not afraid of what's happening in there. You already know the turmoil, the questions, the wounds, the fears. Today I'm choosing soul honesty over spiritual performance. I bring You the real condition of my inner life. Like David, I'm learning to talk to my soul and redirect my hope toward You. Teach me this week how to care for my soul—not just manage it. Heal what's been damaged. Restore what's been depleted. Sanctify me wholly—spirit, soul, and body. In Jesus' name, amen.

Daily Declaration

My soul is where my real story is stored—
and God is not afraid of that story.
Today I practice soul honesty,
bringing Him the truth about what's happening inside.

You are seen. You are loved. You are His.
Body, soul, and spirit—all known by Him.

Quote of the Day
"Your soul doesn't need performance—it needs honesty. God already knows what's there. The question is: will you?"

Day 16 – The Three Control Systems of Your Soul

YOUR SOUL'S COMMAND CENTER: MIND, WILL, AND EMOTIONS

Scripture

"And be not fashioned according to this world: but be ye transformed by the renewing of your mind, that ye may prove what is the good and acceptable and perfect will of God."
—Romans 12:2 (ASV)

"For it is God who worketh in you both to will and to work, for his good pleasure."
—Philippians 2:13 (ASV)

Reflection

Yesterday, you discovered that your soul is where your real story is stored—the hidden, sacred space where nobody else can see what's happening. Today, we're going deeper into understanding how your soul actually works.

Chapter 3 of *Who Am Eye?* teaches that your soul operates through three interconnected systems, like an air traffic control tower managing incoming flights:

Your Mind (Radar System) – gathering and processing information
Your Will (Flight Controller) – making decisions about what gets

permission to "land"

Your Emotions (Weather System) – affecting how everything feels and flows

When these three work together under the Holy Spirit's leadership, you experience peace, clear thinking, and wise decisions. But when there's interference or poor communication between systems, chaos results—and different versions of yourself take control.

Your Mind: The Interpreter

Your mind is where you process information, form opinions, and construct your understanding of reality. But here's what you need to understand: **your mind interprets everything through the lens of what's already stored in your soul.**

If your soul carries wounds of rejection, your mind will interpret neutral situations as personal attacks. If your soul is saturated with shame, your mind will filter every experience through the belief that you're not enough.

As Chapter 3 explains: "Your False Self loves to hijack your mind. It fills your thoughts with lies: 'You'll never change.' 'Nobody really cares about you.' 'You're too broken to be used by God.'"

But when your True Self leads through your spirit connected to God, your mind becomes renewed. Romans 12:2 promises this transformation. A renewed mind doesn't deny reality—it interprets reality through God's truth instead of your pain.

Your Will: The Decision Maker

Your will is your decision-making faculty. It's where you exercise agency and determine the direction of your life. God gave you a will because He made you in His image—you're not a puppet or a robot.

Here's the tension: **your will can be influenced by your mind, driven by your emotions, or surrendered to your spirit.**

When your False Self controls your will, you make choices driven by fear, self-protection, and survival. When your Presentable Self controls your will, you make choices based on image management and approval-seeking.

But when your True Self—anchored in your spirit and connected to God—leads your will, you begin to make choices aligned with who God says you are, not who your pain says you've become.

As your book teaches: "Your will is the bridge between knowing who you are and living like it."

Your Emotions: The Responders

Your emotions add color, texture, and intensity to your experience of life. They react to what your mind believes, what your will chooses, and what your body experiences.

Emotions are not bad—they're God-given. Jesus experienced the full range of human emotion. But **emotions were never meant to be in charge. Emotions are responders, not leaders.**

The problem comes when your emotions hijack the control center:

Fear makes decisions that only God should make

Anger drives you to wound others in your pain

Shame convinces you to hide from the very people who could help you heal

Your False Self uses emotions as evidence: "I feel worthless, therefore I am worthless." Your Presentable Self suppresses emotions: "I can't let anyone see me cry."

But your True Self, led by your spirit, learns to acknowledge emotions without being ruled by them. You can feel afraid and still choose courage. You can feel sad and still trust God's goodness.

When the Systems Go to War

Here's what many of us experience daily: our three control systems go to war with each other.

Your mind says, "You need to forgive them."
Your emotions scream, "But they hurt me!"
Your will freezes, caught in the middle.

This internal war is exhausting. It's why so many believers feel fragmented, divided against themselves, unable to experience the abundant life Jesus promised.

None of these systems were designed to lead. Your spirit, connected to God's Spirit, was always meant to be the leader. When your spirit leads, your mind is renewed, your will is surrendered, and your emotions are submitted to God's truth.

Guided Questions for Reflection

Of the three control systems (mind, will, emotions), which one tends to dominate your daily decisions? Which one gets neglected?

....

....

....

When your systems "go to war," what does that typically look like for you? (Example: knowing what's right but feeling too afraid to do it)

....

....

....

Think of a recent difficult situation. Which self was leading each system? (Mind thinking from fear? Will choosing performance? Emotions driving control?)

....

....

....

What would change if your spirit—connected to God—led all three systems in that situation?

....

....

....

My Thoughts

(Use this space to write any additional personal reflections about today's devotional)

....

....

....

....

Bible Character Reflection

Paul – Throughout his letters, Paul demonstrates what it looks like when the spirit leads the soul's control systems:

Renewed Mind: "I count all things loss for the excellency of the knowledge of Christ" (Philippians 3:8)

Surrendered Will: "Not my will, but Your will be done" (Luke 22:42)

Submitted Emotions: "I am filled with comfort, I overflow with joy in all our affliction" (2 Corinthians 7:4)

Paul's soul wasn't perfect or pain-free. But he had learned to let his spirit—anchored in Christ—lead his mind, will, and emotions back to truth when they started to drift.

Like Paul, your transformation comes from letting the Spirit lead your soul's command center.

Spiritual Practice of the Day

The Control Tower Check-In (10 minutes)

Part 1: Identify Which System is Active (3 minutes)

Right now, which of your three systems is most active?

Am I overthinking? (Mind is overactive)

Am I feeling overwhelmed? (Emotions are flooding)

Am I stuck in indecision? (Will is paralyzed)

Name it honestly.

Part 2: Ask Which Self is Leading (3 minutes)

Now ask: Which version of myself is running this system right now?

Is my False Self thinking fearful thoughts?

Is my Presentable Self managing appearances?

Is my Actual Self honestly processing struggle?

Is my True Self anchored in God's truth?

Part 3: Invite the Spirit to Lead (4 minutes)

Pray: "Holy Spirit, I've been letting [name the system] run the show. I've been operating from [name the self]. I surrender this system to Your leadership. Renew my mind with Your truth. Align my will with Your purposes. Bring peace to my emotions. Help me live from my True Self today."

Wait. Listen. Write what shifts.

Prayer

Father, thank You for creating my soul with these three beautiful systems—mind, will, and emotions. I confess that I've let them war against each other instead of working in harmony under Your Spirit's leadership. I've let my False Self hijack my thoughts, my Presentable Self control my choices, and my emotions dictate my direction. Today I'm choosing to let my spirit—connected to Your Spirit—lead my soul's command center. Renew my mind with Your truth. Surrender my will to Your purposes. Bring peace to my emotions. Teach me what it means to live from my True Self, anchored in Your unchanging love. In Jesus' name, amen.

Daily Declaration

My soul has three control systems— mind, will, and emotions— but my spirit, connected to God's Spirit, was designed to lead them all. Today I choose alignment over chaos, truth over fear, surrender over control.

You are seen. You are loved. You are His.

Body, soul, and spirit—all being transformed by grace.

Quote of the Day

"The soul's three systems were never meant to fight each other. They were designed to work in harmony under the Holy Spirit's leadership—your mind renewed, your will surrendered, your emotions at peace."

Day 17 – When Your Soul Gets Hijacked

Recognizing When Fear Takes the Controls

Scripture

"For God hath not given us the spirit of fear; but of power, and of love, and of a sound mind."

—2 Timothy 1:7 (KJV)

"The thief cometh not, but for to steal, and to kill, and to destroy: I am come that they might have life, and that they might have it more abundantly."

—John 10:10 (KJV)

Reflection

For the past two days, you've been learning about your soul—where your real story is stored (Day 15) and how its three control systems work together (Day 16). Today we face a sobering reality: **what happens when your soul gets hijacked.**

Chapter 3 of *Who Am Eye?* explains: "When trauma hijacks the radar system, it becomes overactive and unreliable. It starts giving the flight controller false readings, detecting threats that may not actually exist. This causes overreaction in the control tower—every blip on the screen looks like danger."

This is often when your False Self takes over—you become defensive before anyone attacks, suspicious when people are trying to help, or controlling when surrender would bring peace.

The Enemy's Strategy

Satan doesn't need to destroy you to win—he just needs to hijack your soul's control systems. Here's his strategy:

He attacks your mind with lies about your identity
He manipulates your will through fear and shame
He overwhelms your emotions with anxiety and despair

Remember Genesis 3? Satan didn't attack Eve's body first—he went straight for her soul. He twisted God's words, contradicted His truth, and planted seeds of doubt. When Eve and Adam disobeyed, their perception of themselves and God changed dramatically.

As your book explains: "I believe this was the moment their souls were traumatized by the knowledge of evil, and they began to hide, blame, and distort reality—patterns we still struggle with today."

Signs Your Soul Has Been Hijacked

How do you know when your soul's control systems have been taken over? Watch for these patterns:

Hijacked Mind:

Obsessive thoughts you can't turn off

Constant replay of past failures

Catastrophic thinking about the future

Interpreting everything through fear

Hijacked Will:

Paralyzed by indecision

Making choices from panic, not peace

Unable to set healthy boundaries

Choosing control over trust

Hijacked Emotions:

Emotional numbness or emotional flooding

Reactions that don't match the situation

Feelings driving all your decisions

Unable to feel God's presence

Which Self Takes Over When You're Hijacked

When your soul gets hijacked, different versions of yourself rush in to take control:

False Self becomes the crisis manager—using old survival strategies that once protected you but now sabotage your peace.

Presentable Self goes into damage control—working overtime to make sure nobody sees you're falling apart.

Actual Self gets buried—your honest struggle can't surface because the emergency response team is running the show.

True Self gets disconnected—the version of you that's secure in God's love feels unreachable.

The Path Back to Peace

Here's the hope: **a hijacked soul can be reclaimed.** But it requires recognizing what's happened and inviting the Holy Spirit back into the control tower.

As Chapter 3 teaches: "In Christ, we have authority to stand against these lies and choose to live from our truest identity."

The reclaiming process involves:

Recognize - "My soul has been hijacked. This isn't my True Self responding."

Pause - Stop reacting and take three deep breaths.

Reconnect - "Holy Spirit, I need You back at the helm."

Redirect - Ask: "What would my True Self—anchored in God's love—do here?"

Guided Questions for Reflection

What situations or triggers tend to hijack your soul's control systems most quickly? (Criticism? Conflict? Uncertainty? Rejection?)

....

....

....

When your soul gets hijacked, which self typically takes over? (False Self protecting? Presentable Self performing? Or do you shut

down completely?)

....

....

....

Think of a recent time your soul was hijacked. Looking back, what were the warning signs you missed?

....

....

....

What would it look like to invite the Holy Spirit back into your control tower before a full hijacking occurs?

....

....

....

My Thoughts

(Use this space to write any additional personal reflections about today's devotional)

....

....

....

....

Bible Character Reflection

Peter in the Garden – When soldiers came to arrest Jesus, Peter's soul got hijacked by fear and his False Self took over:

Hijacked Will: Drew his sword and attacked (John 18:10)

Hijacked Mind: Forgot everything Jesus had taught about the Father's plan

Hijacked Emotions: Acted from panic instead of trust

But Jesus didn't condemn Peter's hijacked response—He gently restored him: "Put up thy sword" (John 18:11). Later, after the resurrection, Jesus gave Peter three opportunities to declare his love, reclaiming what had been hijacked by fear.

Like Peter, your hijacked moments don't disqualify you from God's love. They're opportunities for deeper surrender.

Spiritual Practice of the Day

The Hijacking Alert System (Throughout the day)

Set three alarms on your phone today at different times. When each alarm goes off, do this quick check:

Alert 1: Body Check – Where am I holding tension? (Clenched jaw? Tight shoulders? Shallow breathing?)

Alert 2: Mind Check – What thoughts are on repeat? Are they true, or are they fear-based?

Alert 3: Spirit Check – Do I feel connected to God right now, or has something hijacked my peace?

If you notice hijacking happening, use the 4 R's:

Recognize it

Pause before reacting

Reconnect with the Holy Spirit

Redirect from your True Self

Prayer

Father, I confess that my soul has been hijacked more often than I've realized. The enemy has been attacking my mind with lies, manipulating my will through fear, and overwhelming my emotions with anxiety. I've let my False Self and Presentable Self take control when things get difficult. But today I'm choosing to reclaim my soul's control tower. Holy Spirit, I invite You back to the helm. Alert me when hijacking is beginning. Give me the courage to pause, recognize what's happening, and reconnect with You before I react from a hijacked place. Teach me to live from my True Self—the version of me that's secure in Your unchanging love. In Jesus' name, amen.

Daily Declaration

When my soul gets hijacked, I don't have to stay in that place. I can recognize, pause, reconnect, and redirect. The Holy Spirit is ready to reclaim what the enemy tried to steal.

You are seen. You are loved. You are His.

Even when hijacked, you can return to His peace.

Quote of the Day

"A hijacked soul feels like chaos, but it's actually your invitation to surrender control back to the One who never panics—the Holy Spirit who specializes in bringing peace to inner storms."

Day 18 – Emotions: Data, Not Directives

Learning to Feel Without Being Controlled by Feelings

Scripture

"Be ye angry, and sin not: let not the sun go down upon your wrath."

—Ephesians 4:26 (KJV)

"Let every man be swift to hear, slow to speak, slow to wrath."

—James 1:19 (KJV)

Reflection

Yesterday you learned what happens when your soul gets hijacked. Today we're going to explore one of the most misunderstood aspects of soul care: **your emotions.**

Chapter 6 of *Who Am Eye?* teaches one of the most liberating truths you'll ever discover: **"Your emotions are data, not directives."**

Let me explain what this means. Your emotions provide valuable information about what's happening in your soul and which version of yourself might be taking over. But they shouldn't automatically drive your decisions or actions.

When you feel angry, that anger is telling you something important—perhaps a boundary has been crossed or an injustice has occurred. But the emotion itself doesn't tell you how to respond. That's where many of us get stuck.

The Problem with Emotional Directives

Many of us were raised in environments where emotions were either:

Completely suppressed – "Real Christians don't get angry/sad/anxious"

Completely in charge – "If you feel it, you must act on it immediately"

Both extremes are unhealthy. God gave you emotions as part of being made in His image. Jesus felt the full range of human emotion—joy, sorrow, anger, compassion, grief.

But emotions were never meant to be your master. They were designed to be messengers, not commanders.

How Emotions Reveal Which Self Is Leading

Here's how emotions serve as helpful data about which version of yourself is emerging:

Reactive anger might signal your False Self (wounded self) is trying to protect you

Performance anxiety might indicate your Presentable Self is taking over, terrified of being exposed

Shame-based hiding might reveal your False Self is in control, convinced you're not worthy of love

Peace in difficulty might show your True Self is leading from God's security

The emotion itself isn't the problem—it's information. The question is: which self is interpreting that information and deciding how to respond?

The David Model: Feel Everything, Trust God Anyway

Look at how David handled emotions in the Psalms:

Raw honesty: "I am weary with my groaning; Every night I make my bed to swim; I water my couch with my tears" (Psalm 6:6)

Fierce anger: "Break their teeth, O God, in their mouth" (Psalm 58:6)

Deep depression: "My tears have been my food day and night, While they continually say unto me, Where is thy God?" (Psalm 42:3)

Overwhelming joy: "Thou hast turned for me my mourning into dancing" (Psalm 30:11)

David felt everything deeply. But notice what he did with those emotions—he brought them to God, acknowledged them honestly, and then redirected his hope toward truth.

He didn't let his feelings have the final word about his identity.

Guided Questions for Reflection

What emotions do you tend to suppress or ignore because you've been taught they're "not spiritual"?

....

....

....

What emotions tend to take over and drive your decisions without any filter?

....

....

....

Think of a recent strong emotion you experienced. What data was it giving you about which self was leading?

....

....

....

How would your relationships change if you could feel deeply without being controlled by those feelings?

....

....

....

My Thoughts

(Use this space to write any additional personal reflections about today's devotional)

....

....

....

....

Bible Character Reflection

Elijah After Mount Carmel (1 Kings 19) – After his greatest victory, Elijah's emotions crashed:

The Data: He felt afraid, exhausted, alone, and wanted to die

The Directive He Almost Took: "I'm done. I quit. It's over."

God's Response: He didn't rebuke Elijah's emotions. He let him rest, fed him, and then gently redirected him: "What are you doing here, Elijah?"

God honored Elijah's emotional data (you're exhausted, you're depleted) without letting those emotions write the ending to his story. Elijah's True Self—the prophet called by God—was still there, even when his emotions were screaming otherwise.

Like Elijah, your emotions tell you what you're experiencing, but God's truth tells you whose you are.

Spiritual Practice of the Day

The Emotion Translation Exercise (10 minutes)

Part 1: Name the Emotion (3 minutes)

What are you feeling right now? Don't spiritualize it yet. Just name it:

Anxious? Angry? Sad? Lonely? Overwhelmed? Numb?

Write it down.

Part 2: What Data Is It Giving? (3 minutes)

Now ask: What is this emotion trying to tell me?

Am I exhausted and need rest?

Has a boundary been crossed?

Am I afraid of something specific?

Am I grieving a loss?

Part 3: Which Self Is Interpreting? (4 minutes)

Ask: Which version of me wants to respond to this emotion?

False Self says: "Protect yourself! React now!"

Presentable Self says: "Hide this! Don't let anyone see!"

True Self says: "Feel it fully, bring it to God, trust His truth"

Now pray: "Father, this emotion is data about my current experience. I bring it to You honestly. Show me how to respond from my True Self, not from fear or performance."

Prayer

Father, thank You for creating me with emotions. I confess I've either suppressed them completely or let them run my life. I've been afraid to feel deeply because I thought it meant I was failing spiritually. Or I've let my feelings dictate every decision without filtering them through Your truth. Today I'm choosing a different path—the path of emotional honesty guided by spiritual wisdom. Teach me to feel everything, process it with You, and respond from my True Self. Help me see my emotions as data about my soul's condition, not directives about my identity. In Jesus' name, amen.

Daily Declaration

My emotions are messengers, not masters. They tell me what I'm experiencing, but God's truth tells me whose I am. Today I choose to feel deeply while living from my True Self.

You are seen. You are loved. You are His.

Your emotions are valid, and God's truth is constant.

Quote of the Day

"God isn't afraid of your emotions. He gave them to you. The question isn't whether you should feel—it's whose voice gets to interpret what those feelings mean."

Day 19 – The Soul as God's Container

WHAT HAPPENS WHEN THE CONTAINER GETS DAMAGED

Scripture

"Create in me a clean heart, O God; and renew a right spirit within me."
—Psalm 51:10 (KJV)

"He healeth the broken in heart, and bindeth up their wounds."
—Psalm 147:3 (KJV)

Reflection

We've been exploring your soul all week—understanding it as your processing center (Day 15), learning how its three control systems work (Day 16), recognizing when it gets hijacked (Day 17), and yesterday discovering that emotions are data, not directives (Day 18).

Today we look at something crucial: **what happens when your soul's container gets damaged.**

Dr. Rob Reimer teaches a beautiful truth that your book quotes in Chapter 8: "The soul functions like a container designed to hold God's love and truth. At birth, our soul is pure—unstained by toxic relationships, trauma, or sin. But as life unfolds, we encounter experiences that leave deep impressions."

Think of your soul as a sacred vessel. When it's whole and functioning as designed, it holds God's truth, processes life through His perspective, and overflows with His love. But when the container gets cracked or contaminated, everything changes.

How the Container Gets Damaged

Your soul's container can be damaged through:

Trauma – Experiences that overwhelm your ability to process them normally

Toxic relationships – People who consistently shame, manipulate, or abuse

Repeated rejection – Patterns that teach you you're not worthy of love

Unprocessed grief – Loss that was never properly mourned

Generational patterns – Wounds passed down through family lines

When these experiences happen, especially in childhood, they don't just hurt in the moment—they create cracks in your soul's container. And through those cracks, lies begin to seep in about who you are.

The Leaking Container

Chapter 8 explains what happens when your soul's container is damaged: "When the container is damaged through pain, betrayal, or trauma, different coping mechanisms develop—some healthy, some not."

A damaged container can't hold what it was designed to hold:

God's love leaks out through cracks of unworthiness

Truth seeps away through holes of shame

Peace drains through fractures of anxiety

Identity spills through breaks of rejection

And what fills the space instead? The lies whispered through those very cracks: "You're too much." "You're not enough." "You'll always be broken." "Nobody really wants you."

The Different Selves and the Damaged Container

Understanding the damaged container helps explain why different versions of yourself emerge:

False Self develops elaborate strategies to protect the damaged container from further harm

Presentable Self works overtime to hide the cracks so nobody sees the leaking

Actual Self can acknowledge both the damage and the hope for restoration

True Self knows the container is being restored by the Master Potter

The Hope of Restoration

Here's the beautiful truth from your book: "God specializes in soul restoration. He doesn't just patch up the cracks—He replaces what was broken with something stronger."

Chapter 3 shares your personal testimony: "I personally experienced how the blood of Christ covered my container on the inside. Where there were holes, they were completely covered. My soul is no longer leaking empty. The abiding presence of the Holy Spirit now fills me with God's joy and peace."

This is the hope we're anchoring in today: **Your damaged container can be completely restored.** Not just patched, not just managed—fully healed by the One who specializes in making broken things whole.

Guided Questions for Reflection

What early life experiences might have created cracks in your soul's container?

....

....

....

What lies have been seeping in through those cracks? (I'm worthless, I'm too much, I'm not enough, I'll always be alone)

....

....

....

Where have you seen God beginning to restore what was damaged in your soul?

....

....

....

What would your life look like if your soul's container was completely whole and holding God's love without any leaking?

....

....

....

My Thoughts

(Use this space to write any additional personal reflections about today's devotional)

....

....

....

....

Bible Character Reflection

The Woman at the Well (John 4) – Her soul's container had been damaged through:

Multiple broken relationships (five husbands)

Community rejection (coming to the well alone at noon)

Shame that kept her hiding

Searching for love in all the wrong containers

But Jesus saw past her damaged container to her True Self—a worshiper who would worship in spirit and truth. He didn't condemn the cracks; He offered to fill her with living water that would never run dry.

One conversation with Jesus, and her container began to be restored. She went from hiding to proclaiming, from shame to testimony.

Like her, your damaged container doesn't disqualify you from God's restoration. It positions you for His living water.

Spiritual Practice of the Day

The Container Prayer (15 minutes)

Find a quiet place and hold an empty cup or bowl in your hands.

Part 1: Acknowledge the Damage (5 minutes)

Look at the container in your hands and pray: "Father, my soul's container has been damaged by [name specific wounds, relationships, traumas]. These experiences created cracks where lies have seeped in. I've been trying to hold Your love, but it keeps leaking out through holes of unworthiness and shame."

Be honest. Name what damaged your container.

Part 2: Invite Restoration (5 minutes)

Now pray: "But You are the Master Potter. You specialize in restoring broken containers. I invite You to seal every crack with the blood of Christ. Fill every hole with Your healing presence. Restore what was damaged. Make my soul whole again—able to hold Your love without leaking."

Part 3: Receive the Filling (5 minutes)

Imagine God pouring His love, truth, and peace into your container. See it filling up, not leaking out. Feel the weight of being filled.

Pray: "Holy Spirit, fill my restored container with Your presence. Let me overflow with what I've received—not from a damaged place, but from a healed one."

Prayer

Father, my soul's container has been damaged by life's wounds. I've tried to hide the cracks, tried to manage the leaking, tried to pretend I was whole when I was broken. But today I'm bringing You my damaged container with complete honesty. You're not surprised by the holes. You're not disappointed by the fractures. You specialize in restoration. Seal every crack with the blood of Christ. Fill every hole with Your healing presence. Make me whole—able to hold Your love without shame leaking it away. Transform my soul from a damaged container into a vessel of honor, fit for Your glory. In Jesus' name, amen.

Daily Declaration

My soul is God's container, and He specializes in restoration. Where there were cracks, He seals. Where there were holes, He fills. I am being made whole.

You are seen. You are loved. You are His.

Your damaged container is becoming His masterpiece.

Quote of the Day

"God doesn't discard damaged containers—He restores them into vessels of honor. Your cracks become the very places where His light shines through most beautifully."

Day 20 – Soul Care: Bringing Your Brokenness to the Healer

The Path from Damaged to Restored

Scripture

"The Lord is nigh unto them that are of a broken heart; and saveth such as be of a contrite spirit."
—Psalm 34:18 (KJV)

"He sent his word, and healed them, and delivered them from their destructions."
—Psalm 107:20 (KJV)

Reflection

All week you've been exploring your soul—understanding its three control systems, recognizing when it gets hijacked, learning that emotions are data, and yesterday discovering that your soul is like a container that can be damaged but also restored.

Today we come to the most practical question: **How do I actually bring my broken soul to the Healer for restoration?**

Chapter 3 of *Who Am Eye?* provides a clear path: "Soul healing happens when we: Bring our wounds into the light of God's truth, Recognize which versions of the self developed as coping mechanisms, Renounce the lies we've believed about ourselves, Receive God's love in the broken places, Forgive those who hurt us (and ourselves), Choose to live from our truest identity rather than our protective patterns."

This isn't a one-time event—it's an ongoing journey of soul care. Not soul management, but actual deep care of your inner life with the Master Healer.

Step 1: Bring Your Wounds into the Light

The first step in soul healing is the hardest: **honesty about your brokenness.**

Your False Self wants to hide the damage. Your Presentable Self wants to minimize it. But your True Self—anchored in God's love—can bring the full truth into His light.

As John 3:20-21 teaches, *"Everyone who does evil hates the light,* ***and will not come into the light for fear that their deeds will be exposed.*** *But whoever lives by the truth comes into the light, so that it may be seen plainly that what they have done has been done in the sight of God."*

Soul care begins with this prayer: "Father, this is the real condition of my soul. I'm not pretending anymore. Here are my wounds. Here's my brokenness. I bring it all into Your light."

Step 2: Recognize Your Coping Mechanisms

The second step is recognizing which versions of yourself developed to protect your damaged soul:

False Self developed protective walls—"If I control everything, I won't get hurt again"

Presentable Self developed performance strategies—"If I look perfect, maybe I'll finally be accepted"

These weren't wrong at the time—they were survival. But what helped you survive childhood sabotages your ability to thrive as an adult.

Soul care means acknowledging: "These patterns served a purpose once, but they're not who I really am. They're not my True Self."

Step 3: Renounce the Lies

The third step is actively breaking agreement with the lies that seeped in through your soul's damaged container:

"I renounce the lie that I'm worthless."

"I renounce the lie that I'll always be rejected."

"I renounce the lie that I'm too broken to be loved."

"I renounce the lie that God is disappointed in me."

This isn't just positive thinking—this is spiritual warfare. You're taking back ground the enemy gained when your soul was wounded.

Step 4: Receive God's Love in the Broken Places

The fourth step is the most tender: **letting God's love reach the specific places that were damaged.**

This is where many of us struggle. We can receive God's love in general, but we keep His love away from our most broken places—the shame, the abuse, the rejection, the trauma.

Soul care means praying: "Father, I specifically invite Your love into [name the broken place]. Not just comfort, but actual healing. Restore what was damaged here. Fill this crack with Your presence."

Step 5: Forgive and Release

The fifth step involves the hard work of forgiveness:

Forgiving others who damaged your soul's container

Forgiving yourself for how you've responded from your wounds

Releasing your right to revenge or repayment

This doesn't minimize what happened. It releases you from carrying the weight of unforgiveness, which only damages your soul further.

Step 6: Choose Your True Self Daily

The final step is the ongoing practice: **daily choosing to live from your True Self rather than your wounded patterns.**

Every morning: "Today I choose to live from who God says I am, not from my protective mechanisms."

Every difficult moment: "My True Self—secure in God's love—can handle this without reverting to old patterns."

Guided Questions for Reflection

What specific broken place in your soul needs God's healing touch today?

....

....

....

Which coping mechanism (False Self or Presentable Self pattern) has served you longest, and what would it cost you to let it go?

....

....

....

Who do you need to forgive to release your soul from the weight of bitterness?

....

....

....

What would living from your True Self look like in your most challenging relationship?

....

....

....

My Thoughts

(Use this space to write any additional personal reflections about today's devotional)

....

....

....

....

Bible Character Reflection

Naomi/Mara (Ruth 1) – When Naomi returned to Bethlehem after losing her husband and sons, she said: "Call me not Naomi [pleasant], call me Mara [bitter]: for the Almighty hath dealt very bitterly with me" (Ruth 1:20).

Her soul's container had been damaged by devastating loss. She was honest about her brokenness—"I went out full, and the Lord hath brought me home again empty."

But God didn't leave her in that bitter place. Through Ruth's faithfulness and Boaz's kindness, God restored what seemed permanently broken. The woman who said she was empty became full again—grandmother to Obed, great-grandmother to David, ancestor of Jesus.

Like Naomi, your current brokenness is not your final chapter. The Healer specializes in restoration stories.

Spiritual Practice of the Day

The Six-Step Soul Care Prayer (20 minutes)

Walk through all six steps with one specific wound:

1. Bring to Light (3 minutes):

"Father, I bring You this specific wound: [name it]. This is how it damaged my soul's container: [describe it]."

2. Recognize Patterns (3 minutes):

"Because of this wound, I developed these protective patterns: [name your False/Presentable Self strategies]."

3. Renounce Lies (3 minutes):

"I renounce these specific lies that came through this wound: [name them one by one]."

4. Receive Love (4 minutes):

"Father, I invite Your healing love specifically into this broken place. Fill this crack with Your presence. Restore what was damaged."

5. Forgive (4 minutes):

"I choose to forgive [person/situation] for this wound. I release my right to revenge. I also forgive myself for how I've responded from this broken place."

6. Choose True Self (3 minutes):

"Today I choose to live from my True Self in this area. When this wound gets triggered, I will respond from Your love, not from my protective patterns."

Prayer

Father, thank You that You're not intimidated by my brokenness. You've been waiting for me to bring my damaged soul to You for healing. Today I'm choosing soul care over soul management. I bring You my wounds, my protective patterns, my lies, my unforgiveness—all of it. I receive Your healing love in the specific places that were damaged. I choose to forgive those who hurt me and to forgive myself for how I've responded. Teach me to live from my True Self daily, anchored in Your unchanging love rather than my changing circumstances. Make my soul whole again. In Jesus' name, amen.

Daily Declaration

My soul is not beyond repair. The Master Healer specializes in restoration. Today I bring my brokenness to Him and receive His healing in return. I am being made whole.

You are seen. You are loved. You are His.

Your broken soul is becoming His healed masterpiece.

Quote of the Day

"Soul care isn't about pretending you're not broken—it's about bringing your brokenness to the only One who can make you whole."

Day 21 – Sacred Pause: Listening to What Your Soul Is Processing

WEEK 3 INTEGRATION—YOUR SOUL'S STORY

Scripture

"And the very God of peace sanctify you wholly; and I pray God your whole spirit and soul and body be preserved blameless unto the coming of our Lord Jesus Christ."
—1 Thessalonians 5:23 (KJV)

"Search me, O God, and know my heart: try me, and know my thoughts: And see if there be any wicked way in me, and lead me in the way everlasting."
—Psalm 139:23-24 (KJV)

Reflection

Welcome to your Week 3 Sacred Pause—a time to integrate everything you've learned about your soul this week.

You've discovered that:

Your soul is where your real story is stored (Day 15)

Your soul has three control systems: mind, will, emotions (Day 16)

Your soul can get hijacked by fear and wounds (Day 17)

Your emotions are data, not directives (Day 18)

Your soul is like a container that can be damaged and restored (Day 19)

Soul care requires bringing your brokenness to the Healer (Day 20)

Today is not about learning something new—it's about listening deeply to what your soul has been processing all week.

The Integration Question

Here's the central question for today's reflection: **What is the current condition of my soul, and what is God inviting me to do about it?**

Not what your soul *should* be like. Not how spiritual you *appear* to be. But the real, honest condition of your inner life right now.

Is your soul...

Peaceful or anxious?

Rested or exhausted?

Hopeful or despairing?

Honest or hiding?

Healing or still bleeding?

Processing or avoiding?

David's Practice Revisited

Remember how David talked to his soul throughout the Psalms? Today you're going to practice that same soul conversation—but this time, you're integrating a full week of discovery.

David modeled three movements:

1. Honest Assessment – "Why are you cast down, O my soul?" (Psalm 42:5)

2. Truthful Redirect – "Hope in God" (Psalm 42:5)

3. Confident Declaration – "For I shall again praise him, my salvation and my God" (Psalm 42:5-6)

You're going to walk through these same three movements today.

Week 3 Integration Practice

Part 1: Honest Soul Assessment (10 minutes)

Answer these questions without filtering or spiritualizing:

Which of my three soul systems (mind, will, emotions) is most out of alignment right now?

....

....

What specific wound or damage in my soul's container needs the most healing attention?

....

....

Which version of myself (Actual, False, Presentable, True) has been showing up most consistently this week?

....

....

What lies have been seeping in through cracks in my soul's container?

....

....

What emotions have I been treating as directives instead of data?

....

....

Part 2: Truthful Redirect (10 minutes)

Now, like David, redirect your soul toward truth. For each area of struggle you identified above, write God's truth:

Where my mind is anxious, God's truth is:

....

....

Where my will is paralyzed, God's truth is:

....

....

Where my emotions are flooding, God's truth is:

....

....

Where my soul feels damaged, God's truth is:

....

....

Part 3: Confident Declaration (5 minutes)

Now complete this declaration, filling in what God has shown you this week:

"O my soul, though you have been [describe your struggle], I choose to hope in God. He is sanctifying me wholly—spirit, soul, and body. This week I discovered that [name one key insight]. Because of this truth, I shall again praise Him. He is my salvation and my God."

Write your personalized declaration here:

....

....

....

....

Guided Questions for Deeper Integration

Looking back over Week 3, what was the most uncomfortable truth you had to face about your soul's condition?

....

....

....

Where did you see evidence of soul healing beginning to happen this week?

....

....

....

Which day's devotional spoke most directly to where you are right now, and why?

....

....

....

What specific soul care practice do you need to continue beyond this week?

....

....

....

My Thoughts

(Use this space to write any additional personal reflections about Week 3)

....
....
....
....

Bible Character Reflection

Jesus in Gethsemane – Even Jesus practiced soul honesty:

Soul Assessment: "My soul is exceeding sorrowful, even unto death" (Matthew 26:38)

Honest Processing: "O my Father, if it be possible, let this cup pass from me" (Matthew 26:39)

Truthful Redirect: "Nevertheless not as I will, but as thou wilt" (Matthew 26:39)

Jesus didn't pretend His soul wasn't in agony. He brought the full weight of what He was processing to the Father. But He redirected His will toward the Father's purpose.

Like Jesus, your soul's honesty—even about deep struggle—is not a lack of faith. It's the pathway to surrender.

Spiritual Practice of the Day

The Week 3 Letter to Your Soul (30 minutes)

Write a letter to your soul, integrating everything from this week. Use this template:

Dear Soul,

This week I learned that you are [what you discovered about your soul].

I recognize that you have been wounded by [name the damage].

I see that you've been trying to protect yourself through [name False/Presentable Self patterns].

I acknowledge that you've been processing [name the emotions/thoughts].

But here's what I want you to know: [speak God's truth to your soul].

From now on, I commit to caring for you by [name specific soul care practices].

I'm no longer afraid of what's inside you, because God isn't afraid either.

Together with the Holy Spirit, we're going to [vision for healing].

With hope,

[Your name]

Take time to write this fully. Let it be honest, tender, and hopeful.

Prayer for Week 3 Integration

Father, thank You for this week of discovering my soul—the sacred space where my real story is stored. Thank You that You're not afraid of what You find there. You already knew the wounds, the hijacked systems, the damaged container, the swirling emotions. And You chose to love me anyway.

This week I've learned that soul care isn't about pretending I'm fine—it's about bringing You my brokenness and receiving Your healing. I've discovered that my emotions are data, not directives. I've recognized which versions of myself have been running the show when fear takes over. I've seen the cracks in my container and invited You to seal them.

Now I'm asking: complete what You've begun. Sanctify me wholly—spirit, soul, and body. Continue the restoration You've started. Teach me to live from my True Self—the version of me that's secure in Your love. Help me practice daily soul honesty, bringing You what's really happening inside without shame or performance.

Transform my soul from a hijacked control tower into a peaceful sanctuary where Your Spirit leads all three systems—mind, will, and emotions—in perfect harmony.

In Jesus' name, amen.

Daily Declaration

This week I discovered my soul— where my real story is stored, where my control systems can be hijacked or surrendered, where my container can be damaged or restored. Today I choose soul care over soul management, honesty over performance, healing over hiding.

You are seen. You are loved. You are His.

Spirit, soul, and body—being sanctified wholly.

Quote of the Day

"The soul doesn't need you to be perfect. It needs you to be honest. Bring God what's really there, and watch Him transform what you thought was permanently broken."
—Dr. Johan Green

Preparing for Week 4

Next week, you'll journey even deeper—into your **spirit**, the dimension of your being created specifically for communion with God. If the soul is where your story is stored, the spirit is where God's story about you is anchored.

You'll discover:

How your spirit functions as your anchor

The difference between living *for* your spirit vs. living *from* it

How your True Self emerges from your spirit's connection to God

The hope of future transformation

Rest well today. Integration takes time. Let your soul breathe.

Week 4

Spirit - Communion With God (Chapter 4)

Day 22 – Your Spirit: The Anchor That Holds

The Dimension Created for Divine Communion

Scripture

"The spirit of man is the candle of the Lord, searching all the inward parts of the belly."

—Proverbs 20:27 (KJV)

"But he that is joined unto the Lord is one spirit."

—1 Corinthians 6:17 (KJV)

Reflection

Welcome to Week 4—the final week of this devotional journey. For three weeks, you've been building a foundation:

Week 1: Learning to listen to God's voice

Week 2: Understanding your body as His temple

Week 3: Exploring your soul as your processing center

Now we move to the deepest dimension of your being—**your spirit**, the part of you created specifically for communion with God and designed to live with Him eternally.

Chapter 4 of *Who Am Eye?* teaches: "If the soul asks, 'Which version of myself is showing up today?' the spirit declares, 'Whose love am I anchored in, no matter which winds are currently pushing my sails?'"

This is the crucial difference: while your soul processes your human experience and can be wounded or hijacked, your spirit—when surrendered to God—is where your True Self is anchored in unchanging truth.

The Ship Analogy Deepened

Throughout this devotional, we've been using the ocean and ship metaphor. Now we go deeper into understanding your spirit as the anchor:

The Ocean = God's infinite, unchanging love
The Ship = Your soul (thoughts, will, emotions)
The Anchor = Your spirit, connected to God
Captain Holy Spirit = The One who guides your journey

Here's what's revolutionary: while your soul's ship can be tossed by storms of circumstance, criticism, or crisis, **your spirit-anchor holds steady in the ocean floor of God's eternal love.**

You may *feel* like you're drifting (soul experience), but you're actually held firm (spirit reality).

Your Spirit: Three Sacred Functions

Chapter 4 explains that your spirit operates through three key functions:

1. **Intuition (The Anchor's Weight)** – Your spiritual intuition constantly draws you toward truth, creating a pull toward God's reality even when emotions are confused or thoughts are chaotic.

2. **Conscience (The Anchor's Chain)** – Your conscience provides the vital link between your daily life and your spiritual foundation, creating tension when you drift too far from who you really are.

3. **Moral DNA (The Anchor's Flukes)** – God's character is woven into your spirit's fabric. You were designed for righteousness, so sin feels unnatural. You hunger for truth, so deception creates conflict. You long for authentic relationships, so manipulation feels foreign.

These aren't things you achieve—they're already present in your recreated spirit when you're in Christ.

The Revolutionary Truth

Here's what completely transformed my understanding of identity, and what your book emphasizes throughout Chapter 4:

Your spirit is already perfect in Christ.

When you were saved, God didn't just forgive your sins—He recreated your spirit. "Therefore if any man be in Christ, he is a new creature: old things are passed away; behold, all things are become new" (2 Corinthians 5:17).

This means:

Your spirit is already complete

Your spirit is already holy

Your spirit is already one with Christ

Your spirit is already perfectly loved

The journey isn't about *fixing* your spirit—it's about letting your spirit lead your soul and body into alignment with who you already are in Christ.

Why This Changes Everything

For years, I exhausted myself trying to make my spirit more acceptable to God. I was running on empty from spiritual performance. Then I discovered: **my spirit was already complete in Christ.**

The question wasn't how to improve my spirit, but **how to live FROM the security and wholeness I already possessed.**

This is where "Who Am Eye?" meets "Whose Am Eye?" in perfect clarity:

Who Am Eye? = Discovered by living from your spirit's reality

Whose Am Eye? = Settled by your spirit's union with God

When your spirit leads, your True Self emerges naturally—not as something you perform, but as someone you already are.

Guided Questions for Reflection

Have you been trying to *fix* your spirit, or learning to *live from* your spirit's completeness in Christ?

....

....

....

When you think of your spirit as an anchor in God's love, what storms currently threaten to convince you you're drifting?

....

....

....

Of the three spirit functions (intuition, conscience, moral DNA), which one do you most clearly sense operating in your life?

....

....

....

What would change if you truly believed your spirit is already perfect and complete in Christ?

....

....

....

My Thoughts

(Use this space to write any additional personal reflections about today's devotional)

....

....

....

....

Bible Character Reflection

Lazarus After Resurrection (John 11) – When Jesus called Lazarus from the tomb, he didn't come out gradually improving. He came out *alive*—completely restored.

This is what happened to your spirit the moment you were saved. You didn't get a damaged spirit that slowly gets better. You got a completely new spirit, already alive in Christ, already perfect, already one with Him.

Your journey isn't about resurrecting your spirit (that already happened). It's about unwrapping the grave clothes (soul wounds, false patterns, old identities) so your resurrected spirit can lead your whole life.

Like Lazarus, you're already alive. Now you're learning to live like it.

Spiritual Practice of the Day

The Anchor Meditation (15 minutes)

Find a quiet place. Close your eyes and visualize:

Part 1: See the Storm (3 minutes)

Picture your soul as a ship being tossed by current circumstances:

What waves of criticism are hitting your vessel?

What winds of worry are pushing your sails?

What currents of comparison are pulling you off course?

Don't try to calm the storm yet. Just acknowledge it's real.

Part 2: Feel the Anchor (5 minutes)

Now picture your spirit as an anchor dropped deep into the ocean floor of God's love. Feel it holding firm despite the storm above.

Say aloud: "My spirit is anchored in God's unchanging love. The storm is real, but so is the anchor. I am held."

Part 3: Trust the Hold (7 minutes)

Now pray: "Father, thank You that my spirit is already complete in Christ. While my soul processes this storm, my spirit remains anchored in Your love. Teach me to live from this anchored place. Let my True Self—secure in You—lead my whole life today."

Rest in this truth for the remaining time.

Prayer

Father, thank You for creating me with a spirit—the dimension of my being designed specifically for communion with You. Thank You that when I was saved, You didn't just forgive my sins—You completely recreated my spirit. It's already perfect, already complete, already one with Christ.

I confess I've been trying to *fix* my spirit instead of living *from* its completeness. I've been performing for Your approval when I already have it fully. I've been striving to become who I already am in Christ.

Today I'm choosing a different path. I'm accepting that my spirit is my anchor, holding firm in the ocean of Your love regardless of what storms my soul is processing. Teach me to live from this anchored place. Let my True Self—rooted in my spirit's union with You—lead my thoughts, choices, and emotions.

I am Yours. Completely. Eternally. Unshakeably.

In Jesus' name, amen.

Daily Declaration

My spirit is my anchor, holding firm in God's unchanging love. While my soul may be tossed by storms, my spirit remains secure in Christ. I am learning to live FROM this anchored place.

You are seen. You are loved. You are His.

Your spirit is already complete—now live like it.

Quote of the Day

"Your spirit isn't something you perfect—it's the perfected dimension from which you live. Stop trying to fix what God already completed. Start living from what Christ already accomplished."

Day 23 – Three Sacred Functions of Your Spirit

INTUITION, CONSCIENCE, AND MORAL DNA

Scripture

"For what man knoweth the things of a man, save the spirit of man which is in him? even so the things of God knoweth no man, but the Spirit of God."

—1 Corinthians 2:11 (KJV)

"The spirit truly is ready, but the flesh is weak."

—Matthew 26:41 (KJV)

Reflection

Yesterday you discovered that your spirit is the anchor that holds you steady in God's love. Today we explore how that anchor actually *functions*—the three sacred ways your spirit operates to keep you connected to God's truth.

Chapter 4 of *Who Am Eye?* teaches that your spirit works through three key functions, which I illustrated as parts of an anchor:

Intuition (The Anchor's Weight) – drawing you toward truth

Conscience (The Anchor's Chain) – connecting you to your foundation

Moral DNA (The Anchor's Flukes) – gripping God's character

Let's explore each one and how they help your True Self emerge.

Function 1: Spiritual Intuition (The Weight)

Your spiritual intuition is that deep *knowing* that transcends reasoning. It's the pull you feel toward what is right, safe, and aligned with God's heart—even when your mind can't explain it and your emotions are confused.

As your book explains: "Just as an anchor's weight pulls it down toward the ocean floor, your spiritual intuition is constantly drawing you toward truth, always seeking the solid ground of God's reality."

This is *not* the same as your soul's thoughts or feelings. This is deeper—a Spirit-to-spirit communication that bypasses your processing center and speaks directly to your core.

Example from my own journey: There were seasons when I was caught up in trying to please everyone and prove my worth through what I did. During those times, whenever I said yes to things that weren't really what God wanted for me, I'd feel this nagging uneasiness inside. It wasn't guilt about being busy. It was something deeper—my spirit knew I was off track and kept pulling me back toward what was true and right.

Your spiritual intuition is that pull. Learn to recognize it.

Function 2: Conscience (The Chain)

Your conscience is the vital link between your daily life and your spiritual foundation. It creates moral tension when you begin drifting too far from who you really are in Christ.

As Chapter 4 describes: "Just as a ship's captain can feel the tug of the anchor chain when the vessel begins to drift, your conscience creates that moral tension when you begin moving away from who you really are in Christ."

This is crucial: Your conscience operates *from* your True Self, calling you back to who you really are no matter which version of yourself is currently expressed.

When your wounded self wants to retaliate, your conscience whispers mercy.

When your performing self wants to take credit, your conscience points toward humility.

When your hidden self wants to stay isolated, your conscience encourages authentic connection.

Your conscience isn't condemnation—it's the gentle but firm pull that says, "You're drifting. Time to return to your foundation."

Function 3: Moral DNA (The Flukes)

Just as an anchor's flukes are specifically shaped to grip the ocean floor, your moral DNA is woven into the very fabric of your spirit with God's own character patterns.

Here's what this means practically:

You were designed for righteousness – sin feels unnatural because it contradicts your spiritual DNA, even when you're operating from wounded places

You hunger for truth – deception creates internal conflict because lies oppose your nature, even when you're tempted to hide or perform

You long for authentic relationships – manipulation feels foreign to your True Self, even when fear drives you toward self-protection

This divine imprint cannot be altered by circumstances, damaged by trauma, or destroyed by sin. It's permanent. It's who you are at the core.

How These Functions Work Together

When all three functions operate in harmony, something beautiful happens:

Your intuition draws you toward God's truth

Your conscience alerts you when you're drifting from it

Your moral DNA confirms what aligns with who you really are

This is how your True Self naturally emerges—not through striving or performance, but through living from your spirit's connection to God.

When Your Soul Overrides Your Spirit

The tragedy is that many believers live with their soul (mind, will, emotions) overriding their spirit's voice:

Mind drowns out intuition with overthinking

Will ignores conscience to maintain control

Emotions override moral DNA with reactive patterns

This is when False Self and Presentable Self dominate, and True Self gets buried.

But when you learn to let your spirit lead your soul, everything aligns. Your thoughts become clearer, your choices wiser, your emotions more stable—because they're all following the anchor that's already holding firm.

Guided Questions for Reflection

When have you felt your spiritual intuition pulling you toward something, even when your mind couldn't explain why?

....

....

....

What does your conscience keep gently tugging you about? What drift is it trying to correct?

....

....

....

When you do something that violates your moral DNA, what does that internal conflict feel like?

....

....

....

Which function (intuition, conscience, moral DNA) do you most need to start listening to instead of overriding?

....

....

....

My Thoughts

(Use this space to write any additional personal reflections about today's devotional)

....

....

....

....

Bible Character Reflection

Paul on the Road to Damascus (Acts 9) – Before his conversion, Paul's spirit was dead, disconnected from God. His soul ran the show—his mind was convinced he was serving God by persecuting Christians.

But the moment Jesus appeared, Paul's spirit was made alive. Suddenly:

His intuition recognized truth he'd been resisting

His conscience convicted him of being off course

His moral DNA aligned with God's actual character

From that moment forward, Paul lived from his spirit, not his soul. Even when his body was imprisoned, his emotions troubled, or his mind perplexed—his spirit remained anchored in Christ.

Like Paul, your transformation happens when your spirit—made alive in Christ—begins leading your whole life.

Spiritual Practice of the Day

The Three Functions Check-In (15 minutes)

Part 1: Intuition Assessment (5 minutes)

Ask yourself: "What has my spiritual intuition been pulling me toward that I've been resisting?"

Listen quietly. Don't overthink. What deeper knowing keeps surfacing?

Write it down: ....

Part 2: Conscience Examination (5 minutes)

Ask: "What moral tension have I been feeling? What drift is my conscience trying to correct?"

Be honest. Where have you been moving away from your True Self?

Write it down: ....

Part 3: Moral DNA Recognition (5 minutes)

Ask: "What feels 'off' in my life right now—not just inconvenient, but contrary to who I really am at the core?"

Identify what violates your God-given nature.

Write it down:
....

Now pray: "Holy Spirit, thank You for these three sacred functions. Help me stop overriding them. I choose to listen to my intuition, heed my conscience, and honor my moral DNA. Teach me to live from my spirit, not just my soul."

Prayer

Father, thank You for the intricate design of my spirit—three sacred functions that keep me connected to You. Thank You for spiritual intuition that constantly draws me toward truth, for conscience that alerts me when I'm drifting, for moral DNA that confirms what aligns with who I really am.

I confess I've been overriding these functions with my soul's noise. My overthinking mind drowns out intuition. My stubborn will ignores conscience. My reactive emotions override my moral DNA.

Today I'm choosing to let my spirit lead. When intuition pulls me toward something I don't understand, I'll trust it. When conscience creates tension, I'll listen. When something violates my moral DNA, I'll honor that signal.

Teach me what it means to live from my spirit—the dimension You created for communion with You. Let my True Self emerge naturally as I follow the anchor that's already holding firm in Your love.

In Jesus' name, amen.

Daily Declaration

My spirit has three sacred functions: intuition drawing me toward truth, conscience alerting me when I drift, moral DNA confirming who I really am. Today I choose to listen to all three.

You are seen. You are loved. You are His.

Your spirit knows the way home—follow it.

Quote of the Day

"Your spirit's three functions aren't suggestions you can ignore—they're divine GPS coordinates guiding you back to who you really are. Stop overriding the navigation system God built into your soul."

Day 24 – Living From Your Spirit vs. Living For Your Spirit

The Difference Between Striving and Resting

Scripture

"There remaineth therefore a rest to the people of God. For he that is entered into his rest, he also hath ceased from his own works, as God did from his."

—Hebrews 4:9-10 (KJV)

"Are ye so foolish? having begun in the Spirit, are ye now made perfect by the flesh?"

—Galatians 3:3 (KJV)

Reflection

For three days now, you've been discovering your spirit—the anchor that holds (Day 22), its three sacred functions (Day 23), and today we address a distinction that **completely revolutionized my spiritual life:**

The difference between living *FOR* your spirit and living *FROM* your spirit.

Chapter 4 of *Who Am Eye?* shares my personal breakthrough: "For years, I lived *for* my spirit—constantly trying to prove my worth to God through ministry performance, spiritual disciplines, and religious activities. I was trying to strengthen my 'spiritual' version while eliminating my 'fleshly' versions. Then I discovered the freedom of living *from* my spirit—from the security of who I already was in Christ."

This shift changes everything.

Living FOR Your Spirit: The Exhausting Path

When you live *for* your spirit, you operate from the following:

"I must eliminate my struggling/wounded versions"
"I need to perform spiritually to maintain God's love"
"My identity depends on which version of myself shows up"
"If I pray enough, fast enough, serve enough—*then* I'll be spiritual enough"

This is the treadmill of spiritual performance. You're constantly working to *achieve* what you think will make your spirit acceptable to God.

The result? Exhaustion. Burnout. Secret shame when you can't maintain the performance. And ironically, your False Self (driven by fear of failure) and Presentable Self (managing spiritual appearance) end up running the show while your True Self gets buried under the weight of trying.

I spent years on this treadmill. Ministry became burden instead of joy. My relationship with God became performance review instead of intimate communion. I was spiritually exhausted while appearing spiritually successful.

Living FROM Your Spirit: The Liberating Truth

When you live *from* your spirit, you operate from these truths:

"My True Self is secure regardless of my current struggles"
"I operate from my identity as God's beloved child"
"My actions flow from love, not from fear of being the 'wrong' version"
"My spirit is already complete in Christ—now I live from that completeness"

This is the rest that Hebrews 4 promises. You cease from your own works (trying to perfect your spirit) and enter His rest (living from what Christ already accomplished).

The result? Freedom. Joy. Authenticity. And your True Self naturally emerges because you're not striving to create it—you're simply resting in who you already are.

As your book explains: "When I finally learned to live from my spirit instead of for my spirit, ministry became joy instead of burden. My relationship with God became rest instead of striving."

The Galatians 3 Problem

Paul addressed this exact issue with the Galatian church: "Are ye so foolish? having begun in the Spirit, are ye now made perfect by the flesh?" (Galatians 3:3)

Translation: "You started this journey by receiving what Christ did for you. Now you're trying to perfect yourselves through your own effort? How foolish!"

Many of us do the same thing:

We begin by grace (living from what Christ accomplished)

We continue by works (living for spiritual perfection)

But Paul says this is backwards. If you began in the Spirit, continue in the Spirit. If you started by receiving, keep receiving. If you were saved by grace, grow by grace.

The Practical Difference

Living FOR your spirit looks like:

Performing spiritual disciplines to earn God's approval

Hiding struggles because "spiritual people don't struggle"

Exhausting yourself trying to be the right version

Shame when your Actual Self shows weakness

Using ministry as proof of worthiness

Living FROM your spirit looks like:

Practicing spiritual disciplines as overflow of being loved

Honestly acknowledging struggles while anchored in truth

Resting in your True Self's security in Christ

Grace when your Actual Self shows humanity

Serving from fullness, not emptiness

How This Changes Your Four Selves

When you live FROM your spirit instead of FOR it:

Your Actual Self can be honest without shame—"I'm struggling, AND I'm God's beloved"

Your False Self loses power—you don't need protective walls when you're secure in love

Your Presentable Self can relax—you don't need to manage appearance when acceptance is already yours

Your True Self emerges naturally—not as something you achieve, but as someone you already are

Guided Questions for Reflection

In what areas of your life have you been living FOR your spirit (performing to earn) instead of FROM it (resting in what's already yours)?

....

....

....

What spiritual activities exhaust you because you're doing them for approval rather than from acceptance?

....

....

....

If you truly believed your spirit is already complete in Christ, what would you stop striving for?

....

....

....

What would living FROM your spirit's security look like in your most challenging relationship this week?

....

....

....

My Thoughts

(Use this space to write any additional personal reflections about today's devotional)

....

....

....

....

Bible Character Reflection

Martha and Mary (Luke 10:38-42) – These sisters illustrate the difference perfectly:

Martha lived *for*—serving to prove worth, performing to earn approval, anxious about doing enough

Mary lived *from*—resting at Jesus' feet, receiving before doing, secure enough to just be present

Jesus didn't condemn Martha's service. He redirected her motivation: "Martha, Martha, thou art careful and troubled about many things: But one thing is needful: and Mary hath chosen that good part" (Luke 10:41-42).

The "one thing needful" is learning to receive from Jesus *before* doing for Jesus. Mary understood this. She lived from rest, not for approval.

Like Mary, your True Self knows how to receive before performing, to rest before serving, to be before doing.

Spiritual Practice of the Day

The FOR vs. FROM Inventory (20 minutes)

Part 1: Identify Your "FOR" List (7 minutes)

Make a list of spiritual activities or behaviors you're currently doing *for* approval/worthiness:

Prayer (to earn hearing)?

....

Bible reading (to prove dedication)?

....

Service (to feel valuable)?

....

Church attendance (to appear committed)?

....

Part 2: Reimagine as "FROM" (7 minutes)

Now rewrite each one as flowing *from* your already-complete spirit:

Prayer becomes: Conversation with the One who already delights in me

....

Bible reading becomes: Receiving love letters from the One who chose me

....

Service becomes: Overflow of being filled, not effort to fill up

....

Church becomes: Celebration with family, not performance for strangers

....

Part 3: Declare Your New Reality (6 minutes)

Pray: "Father, I've been living FOR my spirit, trying to perfect what You already completed. Today I choose to live FROM my spirit—secure in Christ, already accepted, already loved. I receive Your approval instead of working for it. I rest in Your completion instead of striving for my own. Teach me this new way of living. In Jesus' name, amen."

Prayer

Father, I confess I've been living FOR my spirit instead of FROM it. I've been trying to perfect what You already completed. I've been performing for approval I already have. I've been striving for worthiness You already gave me freely.

This exhausting treadmill ends today. I choose to step off the performance wheel and step into Your rest. My spirit is already complete in Christ. I don't need to strengthen it, fix it, or prove it. I simply need to live from its security.

Teach me what it means to operate from love instead of fear, from fullness instead of emptiness, from rest instead of striving. Let my True Self emerge naturally as I stop performing and start resting in who I already am in You.

Transform my spiritual disciplines from duties that exhaust me into delights that overflow from being loved. Let my service flow from fullness, my worship from gratitude, my obedience from trust.

I am Yours. Completely. Not because I earned it, but because You gave it.

In Jesus' name, amen.

Daily Declaration

I am done living FOR my spirit, trying to perfect what Christ already completed. Today I choose to live FROM my spirit— secure, loved, complete, resting in His finished work. My True Self emerges from rest, not striving.

You are seen. You are loved. You are His.

Your spirit is complete—now live from that truth.

Quote of the Day

"The moment you stop trying to perfect your spirit and start living from its completeness in Christ, is the moment your True Self steps out of hiding and begins leading your whole life."

Day 25 – Your True Self Lives Here

The Secure Foundation of Your Identity

Scripture

"For ye are dead, and your life is hid with Christ in God."
—Colossians 3:3 (KJV)

"I am crucified with Christ: nevertheless I live; yet not I, but Christ liveth in me: and the life which I now live in the flesh I live by the faith of the Son of God, who loved me, and gave himself for me."
—Galatians 2:20 (KJV)

Reflection

For four days now, you've been exploring your spirit—the anchor that holds (Day 22), its three sacred functions (Day 23), the difference between living for it vs. from it (Day 24). Today we arrive at the most liberating truth of all:

Your True Self lives in your spirit, hidden with Christ in God.

This is where the entire journey of "Who Am Eye?" leads—to discovering that your truest identity isn't found by looking inward at your performance, outward at your circumstances, or backward at your history. It's found by looking *upward* to the One who holds your life in His.

Chapter 4 teaches: "Your True Self lives here, already complete and perfect, and eternally secure in Christ. This isn't another version you work to access—it's the foundation from which all transformation flows."

Let this sink in: **Your True Self is not something you create. It's someone you already are when you're anchored in Christ.**

What Makes Your True Self "True"

Your True Self is true because it's rooted in unchanging truth:

Not based on feelings (which fluctuate)
Not based on circumstances (which change)
Not based on performance (which varies)
Not based on others' opinions (which shift)

Instead, it's based on:

Christ's finished work (which is complete)
God's unchanging character (which is faithful)
Your spirit's union with Him (which is eternal)
His declared identity over you (which is settled)

This means your True Self remains constant even when:

Your Actual Self is struggling with weakness

Your False Self is reacting from wounds

Your Presentable Self is managing appearances

The foundation doesn't move. Your True Self—hidden with Christ in God—is as secure as He is.

The Hiddenness That Protects

Notice the Scripture says your life is "*hidden* with Christ in God" (Colossians 3:3). This hiddenness is protective:

Hidden from enemy attack – Satan can't touch what's secured in God
Hidden from human judgment – Others' opinions can't alter what God declares
Hidden from circumstantial threat – External situations can't change internal reality
Hidden from your own sabotage – Even you can't destroy what Christ preserves

Your True Self is hidden in the safest place in the universe—in Christ, in God. Triple-secured. Unshakeable.

The "Nevertheless I Live" Paradox

Paul captures the paradox perfectly in Galatians 2:20: "I am crucified with Christ: nevertheless I live; yet not I, but Christ liveth in me."

Translation of this mystery:

"I am crucified" = My old identity (False Self rooted in sin) is dead

"Nevertheless I live" = But I'm more alive than ever

"Yet not I" = This life isn't self-generated

"But Christ liveth in me" = My True Self is Christ's life expressed through my unique personality

Your True Self is YOU—your unique personality, gifting, story—but powered by Christ's life within you, not by your own striving.

This is why your True Self can express God's character (love, joy, peace, patience) through YOUR unique voice, YOUR specific calling, YOUR particular relationships.

How Your True Self Transforms the Other Selves

When you learn to live from your True Self (anchored in your spirit's union with Christ), something beautiful happens to the other versions:

Your Actual Self finds hope—"I'm struggling, but I'm being transformed"

Your False Self finds healing—wounds lose their controlling power when you're secure in love

Your Presentable Self finds freedom—you can risk authenticity when acceptance is already yours

Your True Self doesn't eliminate the others through condemnation—it transforms them through love.

Living FROM Your True Self Daily

This isn't a theological concept to admire—it's a daily reality to live from:

Morning: "I am hidden with Christ in God. That's my foundation today."

Throughout the day: "Which self is showing up right now? Let me redirect to my True Self."

In conflict: "My True Self—secure in God's love—can handle this without reacting from wounds."

In failure: "My True Self isn't defined by this mistake. I'm still hidden in Christ."

Evening: "Thank You, Father, that my True Self remained secure all day, even when other versions surfaced."

Guided Questions for Reflection

What does it mean to you personally that your True Self is "hidden with Christ in God"?

....

....

....

In what situations do you most forget that your True Self is secure, and start operating from False or Presentable Self instead?

....

....

....

How would your most challenging relationship change if you consistently showed up from your True Self instead of protective versions?

....

....

....

What would living from your True Self look like in your specific calling, work, or ministry?

....

....

....

My Thoughts

(Use this space to write any additional personal reflections about today's devotional)

....

....

....

....

Bible Character Reflection

Paul's Identity Transformation – Compare Saul (before conversion) to Paul (after):

Saul's identity: Rooted in religious performance, tribal status, personal achievement

Paul's True Self: "I am crucified with Christ... Christ liveth in me" (Galatians 2:20)

Paul didn't improve his old identity—he exchanged it for a new one hidden in Christ. His True Self emerged not from better performance but from union with Jesus.

From that foundation, Paul could:

Suffer without losing hope

Face opposition without retaliating

Acknowledge weakness without shame

Love enemies without bitterness

Why? Because his True Self was anchored in Christ, not circumstances.

Like Paul, your True Self transforms how you handle everything life throws at you.

Spiritual Practice of the Day

The Hidden Life Meditation (20 minutes)

Part 1: Visualize the Hiding Place (7 minutes)

Close your eyes. Picture your True Self hidden with Christ in God—three layers of protection:

First layer: Your True Self (the real you God created)
Second layer: Christ (who wraps His identity around yours)
Third layer: God (whose unchanging character surrounds it all)

See this. Feel the security of triple protection.

Part 2: Test the Security (7 minutes)

Now imagine the things that usually shake your sense of identity:

Criticism

Failure

Rejection

Comparison

Circumstances

Watch each one try to penetrate the three layers. See them unable to reach your True Self hidden in Christ in God.

Say aloud: "My True Self is unreachable by anything that's not from God."

Part 3: Live FROM That Place (6 minutes)

Now pray: "Father, this is where I actually live—hidden with Christ in You. This is my True Self's home. Today, help me live FROM this secure place in every situation. When other versions try to take over, remind me where I really live. In Jesus' name, amen."

Prayer

Father, thank You that my True Self lives in the safest place in the universe—hidden with Christ in You. Thank You that this identity can't be touched by enemy attack, human judgment, circumstantial threats, or even my own sabotage.

I confess I've been living as if my identity depends on what I do, how I perform, what others think, or how I feel. I've been operating from versions of myself that emerged from wounds and fear instead of resting in my True Self anchored in You.

Today I'm choosing to live FROM my secure foundation. My True Self is not something I create—it's someone I already am in Christ. Help me stop striving to become and start resting in who I already am.

When my Actual Self struggles, remind me my True Self is secure. When my False Self reacts from wounds, redirect me to my True Self's healing.

When my Presentable Self manages appearances, call me back to my True Self's freedom.

I am crucified with Christ. Nevertheless I live. Yet not I, but Christ lives in me. This is my True Self. This is where I live. This is whose I am.

In Jesus' name, amen.

Daily Declaration

My True Self lives hidden with Christ in God— secure beyond enemy reach, constant beyond circumstantial change, complete beyond performance measure. Today I choose to live FROM this foundation.

You are seen. You are loved. You are His.

Your True Self is hidden in the safest place—now live like it.

Quote of the Day

"Your True Self isn't hiding from you—it's hidden *for* you, protected in Christ where nothing can touch it. Stop searching for what's already secured. Start living from where you actually are."

Day 26 – The Hope of Future Transformation

Your Spirit's Eternal Destiny

Scripture

"Beloved, now are we the sons of God, and it doth not yet appear what we shall be: but we know that, when he shall appear, we shall be like him; for we shall see him as he is."

—1 John 3:2 (KJV)

"For our conversation is in heaven; from whence also we look for the Saviour, the Lord Jesus Christ: Who shall change our vile body, that it may be fashioned like unto his glorious body."

—Philippians 3:20-21 (KJV)

Reflection

For five days, you've been exploring your spirit—the anchor that holds (Day 22), its three sacred functions (Day 23), the difference between living for vs. from it (Day 24), and yesterday discovering that your True Self lives here, hidden with Christ in God (Day 25).

Today we look forward to the ultimate hope: **your spirit's eternal transformation.**

Chapter 4 of *Who Am Eye?* addresses something that fills me with anticipation every time I think about it: "Scripture teaches us that this physical body you inhabit right now—with all its aches, limitations, and struggles—will one day be completely transformed."

But here's what many miss: **it's not just your body that will be glorified. Your entire being—spirit, soul, and body—will be fully transformed into the image of Christ.**

This hope changes how you live today.

What You Are Now vs. What You Will Be

John writes with beautiful honesty: "Now are we the sons of God" (present reality), "and it doth not yet appear what we shall be" (future mystery), "but we know that, when he shall appear, we shall be like him" (certain hope).

Present Reality: You are *already* God's child. Your spirit is *already* complete in Christ. Your True Self is *already* secured.

Future Glory: You will be *completely* like Jesus—not just in character, but in glorified existence. No more struggle between soul and spirit. No more battle with False or Presentable Selves. Just your True Self, fully realized, perfectly expressing Christ.

Certain Hope: This isn't wishful thinking. It's guaranteed by God's faithfulness.

The Mystery Paul Reveals

In 1 Corinthians 15:51-52, Paul calls it a mystery: "Behold, I shew you a mystery; We shall not all sleep, but we shall all be changed, In a moment, in the twinkling of an eye, at the last trumpet: for the trumpet shall sound, and the dead shall be raised incorruptible, and we shall be changed."

Think about what this means:

Instantaneous – "In a moment, in the twinkling of an eye"
Complete – "We shall all be changed"
Eternal – "Raised incorruptible"

Your current struggle with different versions of yourself? Finished.
Your soul's processing of pain and wounds? Healed completely.
Your body's limitations? Transformed into glory.

How Future Hope Transforms Present Living

Here's where theology becomes intensely practical: **knowing your future transformation changes how you handle your current**

struggles.

When your Actual Self is struggling: "This weakness is temporary. I'm being transformed."

When your False Self gets triggered: "This wound won't define me eternally. Healing is coming."

When your Presentable Self exhausts you: "I won't need these masks forever. Authenticity is my destiny."

When your True Self feels buried: "This is who I'm becoming fully. Even now, Christ is forming me."

As your book teaches: "This hope doesn't make you neglect your body; it makes you treasure it even more. You can take good care of yourself, without worrying about every ache, limitation, or imperfection, because you know that who you really are, goes far beyond what your body can or can't do today."

The Already/Not Yet Tension

This is where many believers get confused. We live in the tension of:

Already - Your spirit is already complete in Christ

Not Yet - Your full transformation isn't complete

Already - You are already God's beloved child

Not Yet - You don't yet fully reflect His image

Already - Your True Self is already secure

Not Yet - You don't yet live from it consistently

This tension isn't failure—it's the normal Christian experience. Paul himself acknowledged it: "Not as though I had already attained, either were already perfect: but I follow after" (Philippians 3:12).

The goal isn't to eliminate the tension but to live faithfully within it—celebrating what's already true while anticipating what's still coming.

What This Means for Your Four Selves Today

Understanding your future transformation brings hope to your present struggle:

Actual Self: Your honest acknowledgment of struggle isn't defeat—it's realistic living in the "not yet" while anchored in the "already"

False Self: Your wounded patterns are being healed progressively now and will be eliminated completely then

Presentable Self: Your need to manage appearances will disappear when you're fully transformed into perfect authenticity

True Self: What you glimpse now in moments of surrender, you'll experience continuously in eternity

Guided Questions for Reflection

How does knowing your complete transformation is guaranteed change how you view your current struggles?

....

....

....

What aspect of your future glorification are you most looking forward to? (No more fear? No more shame? No more performance pressure?)

....

....

....

How can the hope of future transformation help you extend more grace to yourself in the "not yet" of today?

....

....

....

If you truly believed you're being transformed day by day toward this glorious future, what would you stop worrying about?

....

....

....

My Thoughts

(Use this space to write any additional personal reflections about today's devotional)

....

....

....

....

Bible Character Reflection

Abraham's Faith in Future Promise (Romans 4:17-21) – Abraham believed God's promise about a future he couldn't yet see: "And being not weak in faith, he considered not his own body now dead... He staggered not at the promise of God through unbelief; but was strong in faith, giving glory to God."

Abraham's present reality (old age, physical limitations) didn't match God's future promise (father of many nations). But his faith in the "not yet" sustained him through the "already" of daily struggle.

Like Abraham, your faith in future transformation can sustain you through present limitations. Your True Self is being formed into Christ's image—the process started, the outcome guaranteed.

Spiritual Practice of the Day

The Future Vision Prayer (20 minutes)

Part 1: Acknowledge Present Reality (5 minutes)

List your current struggles honestly:

My Actual Self struggles with: ....

My False Self reacts from: ....

My Presentable Self exhausts itself by: ....

Don't minimize. Be honest about the "not yet."

Part 2: Envision Future Glory (10 minutes)

Now close your eyes and imagine your complete transformation:

Picture yourself fully like Christ—no more struggle between different selves, no more wounds controlling your reactions, no more need for protective masks. Just your True Self, fully realized, perfectly expressing God's character through your unique personality.

What does this version of you look like?
How does this version love?
How does this version serve?
How does this version worship?

Let this vision fill you with hope.

Part 3: Bridge Present and Future (5 minutes)

Now pray: "Father, I'm living in the tension between 'already' and 'not yet.' My spirit is already complete in Christ, but my full transformation isn't finished. Thank You that You're faithful to complete what You've begun. Help me live today with the hope of tomorrow—extending grace to my struggles while trusting Your transforming work. In Jesus' name, amen."

Prayer

Father, thank You for the hope of future transformation. Thank You that what I am now is not what I will be. Thank You that my current struggle with different versions of myself is temporary—You're transforming me day by day into the image of Christ.

I confess I sometimes get discouraged by the "not yet"—by how slowly transformation seems to happen, by how often my False Self reacts or my Presentable Self performs. I forget that this process takes a lifetime and beyond.

Today I'm choosing to live in the hope of guaranteed transformation. I'm celebrating the "already"—my spirit is complete in Christ, my True Self is secured, my identity is settled. And I'm trusting the "not yet"—You're faithful to complete what You've begun.

When I'm frustrated with my progress, remind me of Your promise.
When I'm exhausted from struggling, renew my hope in future glory.
When I'm tempted to give up, show me how far I've already come.

I am being transformed from glory to glory. The best is yet to come.

In Jesus' name, amen.

Daily Declaration

I am already God's beloved child, and I am not yet fully transformed. I live in this tension with hope, knowing He who began this good work will be faithful to complete it.

You are seen. You are loved. You are His.

Your transformation is guaranteed—keep trusting the process.

Quote of the Day

"The 'not yet' of your struggle doesn't negate the 'already' of your security. You're being transformed—that's a process, not a failure. Trust the God who finishes what He starts."

Day 27 – Your Spirit: God's Inner Sanctuary

THE SACRED SPACE WHERE HE DWELLS

Scripture

"Know ye not that ye are the temple of God, and that the Spirit of God dwelleth in you?"
—1 Corinthians 3:16 (KJV)

"What? know ye not that your body is the temple of the Holy Ghost which is in you, which ye have of God, and ye are not your own?"
—1 Corinthians 6:19 (KJV)

Reflection

We're nearing the end of Week 4, our final week exploring your spirit. You've discovered it's your anchor (Day 22), learned its three sacred functions (Day 23), understood living from vs. for it (Day 24), found your True Self there (Day 25), and glimpsed your future transformation (Day 26).

Today we arrive at perhaps the most intimate truth of all: **Your spirit is God's inner sanctuary—the sacred space where He chooses to dwell.**

Chapter 4 shares my personal breakthrough: "For the longest time, it was difficult for me to truly believe that my spirit could be the inner sanctuary of the Holy Spirit. Because of my past sins, I didn't feel worthy of such a holy God."

Maybe you've felt this too. How can someone with my history, my struggles, my ongoing battles be a dwelling place for the Holy One?

The Sanctuary You Didn't Build

Here's the revolutionary truth: **You didn't make your spirit worthy of God's presence. He did.**

When you were saved:

He cleansed your spirit completely

He made it holy instantly

He moved in permanently

1 Corinthians 6:11 declares: "But ye are washed, but ye are sanctified, but ye are justified in the name of the Lord Jesus, and by the Spirit of our God."

Past tense. Finished work. Done.

Your spirit became God's sanctuary not because you earned it, but because Christ purchased it. Not because you're good enough, but because His blood was sufficient.

My Defining Day Experience

Let me share the story from your book that illustrates this truth powerfully:

"There came a defining day in my life—inside my own supermarket, when a drug lord's gang was waiting outside to end my life. Earlier that morning during my prayer time, I audibly heard the Lord say, 'If you choose business, you are going to die. If you choose Me, I will give you life.'

That day I surrendered it all to Jesus. It was in that moment, falling on my knees in my own store and crying out 'I surrender it all,' that I experienced the presence of the Holy Spirit for the first time in a completely different way. This time I wasn't experiencing His presence from the outside, coming at me from a church building or through someone else's prayer. **This time it came from within—from the very core of my being.**"

This is what it means for your spirit to be God's sanctuary. Not a place you visit (like a church building), but a place you *are*—where He dwells within you, at your very core.

The Gradual Shift from Doubt to Belief

Your book continues: "Over the years, as I've continued to experience His presence, this reality has gradually shifted from doubt to deep belief. I've come to understand that my spirit truly is His place to dwell, to belong, to call His sanctuary of peace."

This shift doesn't happen overnight. You move from:

Knowing theologically ("The Bible says God dwells in me")

↓

Experiencing occasionally ("I felt His presence today")

↓

Believing personally ("My spirit is His sanctuary")

↓

Living consistently ("I walk in awareness of His dwelling")

Most believers get stuck between knowing and experiencing. They believe the doctrine but don't live in the reality.

What Makes Your Spirit a Sanctuary

A sanctuary has specific characteristics. Your spirit as God's dwelling place is:

Holy – Set apart for His purposes alone

Sacred – Treated with reverence and care

Peaceful – Where His calm resides regardless of external storms

Accessible – You can enter His presence anytime

Protected – Guarded by His presence from enemy invasion

This is why your True Self is so secure—it lives in the sanctuary where God Himself dwells.

How This Changes Everything

When you truly grasp that your spirit is God's inner sanctuary:

You stop seeking Him only in external places – He's not just "out there" in heaven or "over there" in church. He's *within* you.

You access His presence instantly – You don't need to work yourself into an emotional state or perform religious rituals. You simply turn inward to where He already dwells.

You live from the inside out – Your True Self (residing in the sanctuary) leads your soul and body, rather than external circumstances controlling your internal state.

You understand your value – If the King of the universe chose your spirit as His dwelling place, you must be infinitely valuable.

When You Feel Unworthy

Here's what to do when the voice whispers, "You're not holy enough to be God's sanctuary":

Remember: Holiness isn't your achievement; it's His gift
Recall: He chose to dwell in you knowing everything about you
Receive: His presence isn't dependent on your perfection
Rest: The sanctuary is maintained by Him, not you

As your book declares: "This understanding completely transformed how I approach the different versions of myself that show up. Instead of trying to eliminate the wounded or performing parts, I learned to live from the security of my spirit's union with God."

Guided Questions for Reflection

Do you truly believe your spirit is God's inner sanctuary, or do you still see Him as mostly "out there" somewhere?

....

....

....

What would change in your daily life if you lived with constant awareness that the Holy Spirit dwells within your spirit?

....

....

....

What makes you feel unworthy of being God's sanctuary, and how does the gospel answer that lie?

....

....

....

How would living from your spirit-sanctuary (inside-out) differ from living from circumstances (outside-in)?

....

....

....

My Thoughts

(Use this space to write any additional personal reflections about today's devotional)

....

....

....

....

Bible Character Reflection

The Tabernacle/Temple Pattern – In the Old Testament, God dwelt in a physical sanctuary—first the tabernacle, then the temple. But notice the pattern:

Outer Court – Where anyone could come (like your body—visible to all)

Holy Place – Where priests ministered (like your soul—where you process)

Holy of Holies – Where God's presence dwelt (like your spirit—His sanctuary)

The Holy of Holies was:

Separated by a veil

Accessible only once a year

Entered only by the high priest

The place of God's manifest presence

But when Jesus died, "the veil of the temple was rent in twain from the top to the bottom" (Matthew 27:51). The way into God's presence was opened permanently.

Now *you* are the temple. Your spirit is the Holy of Holies. And you have constant access because Jesus is your High Priest who opened the way.

Spiritual Practice of the Day

The Inner Sanctuary Prayer

Part 1: Visualize the Sanctuary

Close your eyes. Picture your spirit as a beautiful sanctuary within you—the innermost room where God's presence dwells.

See it as:

Perfectly clean (washed by Christ's blood)

Brilliantly lit (illuminated by God's glory)

Peacefully quiet (a refuge from external noise)

Constantly accessible (always open to you)

Spend time just "seeing" this inner sanctuary.

Part 2: Enter and Worship

Now, in your mind, enter this sanctuary. You don't have to travel anywhere—you simply turn inward to where He already is.

Say: "Holy Spirit, I come into my own spirit where You dwell. This is Your sanctuary. Thank You for choosing to live here."

Worship Him from this place. Not from your mind's thoughts or your emotions' feelings, but from your spirit's sanctuary.

Part 3: Commit to Awareness

Before you end, pray: "Father, help me live with daily awareness that my spirit is Your sanctuary. When I'm tempted to seek You only in external places, remind me You dwell within. When I feel unworthy, remind me You chose this dwelling place knowing everything about me. Teach me to live from this sanctuary—from the inside out. In Jesus' name, amen."

Set a reminder on your phone to go off three times tomorrow: "God's sanctuary is within you right now."

Prayer

Father, I stand in awe that You chose my spirit as Your dwelling place. Not a building made with hands, but the inner sanctuary of my being—the very core of who I am.

I confess I've often treated You as distant, seeking You "out there" when You've been "in here" all along. I've felt unworthy of hosting Your presence, forgetting that You cleansed my spirit and made it holy when You saved me.

Today I receive this truth: my spirit is Your sanctuary. You dwell within me, not because I'm worthy, but because Christ made me worthy. You live at my core, not because I'm perfect, but because Your grace is sufficient.

Teach me to live from this sanctuary. Let my True Self—residing where You dwell—lead my thoughts, choices, and emotions. Help me access Your presence by simply turning inward to where You already are.

Transform my awareness. I am not seeking a God who's far away. I'm communing with a God who's made His home within my spirit. Holy of Holies. Inner sanctuary. Sacred dwelling place.

I am Yours, and You are mine. My spirit is Your home.

In Jesus' name, amen.

Daily Declaration

My spirit is God's inner sanctuary— the Holy of Holies where He chose to dwell. I don't seek Him in distant places; I turn inward to where He already lives. My True Self resides in this sacred space.

You are seen. You are loved. You are His.

The King of Glory dwells within your spirit—live from that reality.

Quote of the Day

"Stop seeking God only in external places—church buildings, worship services, quiet times. Those are good, but He's closer than that. He dwells in your spirit. You are the sanctuary."

Day 28 – Sacred Pause: The Integration of Body, Soul, and Spirit

Your Whole Being

Scripture

"And the very God of peace sanctify you wholly; and I pray God your whole spirit and soul and body be preserved blameless unto the coming of our Lord Jesus Christ."
—1 Thessalonians 5:23 (KJV)

"I beseech you therefore, brethren, by the mercies of God, that ye present your bodies a living sacrifice, holy, acceptable unto God, which is your reasonable service."
—Romans 12:1 (KJV)

Reflection

Welcome to your final Sacred Pause—a time to integrate everything you've learned over these four transformative weeks.

Week 1: You learned to listen to God's voice and your own heart
Week 2: You discovered your body as God's temple
Week 3: You explored your soul as your processing center
Week 4: You uncovered your spirit as your anchor in God

Today, we bring it all together: **body, soul, and spirit working in harmony under the Holy Spirit's leadership.**

This is what 1 Thessalonians 5:23 prays for—not just spiritual growth, not just emotional healing, not just physical health, but *whole* sanctification. Every dimension of your being, preserved and transformed.

The Symphony of Your Being

Think of your three dimensions like instruments in an orchestra:

Body (the percussion) – Provides rhythm, structure, tangible expression

Soul (the strings) – Adds emotion, processing, complex melodies

Spirit (the conductor) – Leads all parts in harmony

When your spirit conducts (connected to the Holy Spirit), your whole being creates beautiful music. When your soul tries to conduct (processing from wounds), you get discord. When your body tries to lead (driven by appetites), you get chaos.

The goal is divine alignment: **Spirit → Soul → Body**

Four Weeks of Discovery Integration

Let's review what you've discovered about each dimension and how they work together:

Week 1 - Listening (Foundation)

You learned to distinguish God's voice from other voices

You discovered that listening is the gateway to transformation

You practiced soul honesty and spiritual attentiveness

Week 2 - Body (Expression)

Your body is God's temple, designed for worship

Your physical presence reveals which self is leading

Your body tells the truth about your internal state

Week 3 - Soul (Processing)

Your soul has three control systems: mind, will, emotions

Your soul can be hijacked or surrendered

Soul care means bringing brokenness to the Healer

Week 4 - Spirit (Anchor)

Your spirit is your anchor in God's unchanging love

Your True Self lives here, hidden with Christ

Your spirit is God's inner sanctuary

How Your Four Selves Show Up in Each Dimension

Understanding how your different selves express through body, soul, and spirit brings everything into focus:

TRUE SELF (Spirit-led)

Body: Relaxed, present, authentic gestures

Soul: Mind renewed, will surrendered, emotions at peace

Spirit: Anchored in God, conducting the symphony

ACTUAL SELF (Honest but struggling)

Body: Shows signs of fatigue or stress honestly

Soul: Processing openly without pretending

Spirit: Connected but aware of the "not yet"

FALSE SELF (Wound-driven)

Body: Tense, defensive posture, protective stance

Soul: Mind replaying trauma, will controlling, emotions reactive

Spirit: Disconnected from leading role

PRESENTABLE SELF (Image-managing)

Body: Carefully curated appearance, performative gestures

Soul: Mind obsessing over perception, will pleasing, emotions suppressed

Spirit: Ignored in favor of external management

The Integration Question

Here's the central reflection for today: **In which dimension (body, soul, or spirit) do I most need integration, and which self has been dominating that dimension?**

Take time with this. The answer reveals where your next growth step lies.

Comprehensive Integration Practice

Part 1: Body Assessment (5 minutes)

Answer honestly:

What is my body telling me about my internal state right now?

....

Which self shows up most in my physical presence?

....

How well am I caring for God's temple?

....

Part 2: Soul Assessment (5 minutes)

Of my three soul systems (mind, will, emotions), which is most out of alignment?

....

What wounds still hijack my soul's processing?

....

Which self dominates my soul's responses?

....

Part 3: Spirit Assessment (5 minutes)

Am I living FROM my spirit or FOR my spirit?

....

How connected do I feel to my True Self anchored in God?

....

Do I experience my spirit as God's sanctuary?

....

Part 4: Integration Prayer

Now pray through each dimension:

"Father, sanctify my BODY wholly—let it be Your temple, expressing my True Self through authentic presence..."

"Father, sanctify my SOUL wholly—renew my mind, surrender my will, bring peace to my emotions..."

"Father, sanctify my SPIRIT wholly—keep me anchored in You, living from my True Self, aware of Your sanctuary within..."

Part 5: Wholeness Declaration

Complete this declaration:

"I am body, soul, and spirit—created as a whole being. This month I discovered [key insight]. My next step toward wholeness is [specific action]. I commit to living from my True Self by [daily practice]."

Write your personalized declaration:

....

....

....

Guided Questions for Deeper Integration

Looking back over all four weeks, what was the single most transformative truth you discovered?

....

....

....

In which dimension (body, soul, spirit) did you experience the most breakthrough this month?

....

....

....

Which of your Four Selves (Actual, False, Presentable, True) do you now recognize most quickly when it emerges?

....

....

....

What specific practice from these 28 days will you continue as part of your ongoing spiritual formation?

....

....

....

My Thoughts

(Use this space to write any additional personal reflections about your 28-day journey)

....

....

....

....

Bible Character Reflection

Jesus' Perfect Integration – Jesus is our model of perfect body-soul-spirit alignment:

Body: He got tired, hungry, thirsty—yet His body perfectly expressed the Father's love through healing touch, welcoming embrace, and ultimately sacrificial death

Soul: He felt the full range of human emotion—joy, sorrow, anger, compassion—yet His mind stayed renewed, His will surrendered, His emotions guided by truth

Spirit: Constantly communing with the Father, never disconnected, always living from His True Self

Jesus shows us what whole sanctification looks like: every dimension working in perfect harmony under the Spirit's leadership.

Like Jesus, you're being formed into this same integration—body, soul, and spirit all expressing your True Self.

Spiritual Practice of the Day

The Whole Being Surrender

Find a quiet place where you can physically move through this practice.

Body Surrender

Stand and physically present your body to God:

Raise your hands: "My hands are Yours"

Touch your head: "My mind is Yours"

Place hand on heart: "My emotions are Yours"

Kneel: "My whole body is Your temple"

Soul Surrender

Sit and walk through each system:

"I surrender my MIND to be renewed by Your truth"

"I surrender my WILL to be aligned with Your purposes"

"I surrender my EMOTIONS to be guided by Your peace"

Spirit Affirmation

Be still and simply rest in your spirit's reality:

"My spirit is anchored in You"

"My True Self lives here"

"You dwell in my inner sanctuary"

"I am whole in You"

Prayer for Complete Integration

Father, thank You for these 28 days of discovery. Thank You for revealing how You created me as a whole being—body, soul, and spirit—each dimension designed to work in harmony under Your Spirit's leadership.

I present myself to You completely:

My BODY – I surrender it as Your temple. Use my physical presence to express Your love. Heal what's been damaged. Strengthen what's been weakened. Let my body tell the truth about the transformation happening within.

My SOUL – I surrender my mind to be renewed, my will to be aligned, my emotions to be at peace. Heal the wounds that hijack my processing. Restore what's been damaged. Transform my soul into a sanctuary of Your truth.

My SPIRIT – Thank You that it's already complete in Christ. Thank You that my True Self lives here, anchored in Your love. Thank You that You've made my spirit Your dwelling place. Teach me to live FROM this reality daily.

Sanctify me wholly—body, soul, and spirit. Preserve me blameless until Christ returns. Complete the good work You've begun. I am Yours, completely and eternally.

In Jesus' name, amen.

Daily Declaration

I am body, soul, and spirit— a whole being created for God's glory. My spirit anchors me in His love, my soul processes from His truth, my body expresses His presence. I am being sanctified wholly.

You are seen. You are loved. You are His.

Body, soul, and spirit—all being made whole.

Quote of the Day

"You're not just a spirit trapped in a body. You're not just a soul trying to survive. You're a whole being—body, soul, and spirit—created to reflect God's image through every dimension of who you are."

Preparing for the Final Two Days

Tomorrow and the next day, you'll step into the culmination of this entire journey—bringing everything together and declaring your new beginning. These aren't just more devotionals; they're your launch pad into living daily from your True Self.

Rest well tonight. Integration takes time. You've come so far.

Day 29 – Bringing It All Together: The Whole You

From Discovery to Declaration

Scripture

"I therefore, the prisoner of the Lord, beseech you that ye walk worthy of the vocation wherewith ye are called."

—Ephesians 4:1 (KJV)

"For we are his workmanship, created in Christ Jesus unto good works, which God hath before ordained that we should walk in them."

—Ephesians 2:10 (KJV)

Reflection

You've reached Day 29—the penultimate day of this transformative journey. Tomorrow you'll step into your new beginning, but today is about integration and celebration. Today you bring together everything you've discovered about **who you are** and **whose you are**.

Over these 28 days, you've journeyed through:

Learning to listen to God's voice and your own heart

Understanding your body as His sacred temple

Exploring your soul as your processing center

Discovering your spirit as your anchor in God

You've identified your **Four Selves**—Actual, False, Presentable, and True—and learned to recognize which one shows up in different situations.

But most importantly, you've discovered that your **True Self** isn't something you create through performance or perfect through striving. It's **someone you already are** when you're anchored in Christ, hidden with Him in God.

The Question That Started Everything

Remember where we began? The fundamental question: **"Who Am Eye?"**

But you've learned that this question can only be answered through another: **"Whose Am Eye?"**

Who Am Eye? = Discovered through living from your True Self

Whose Am Eye? = Settled by your spirit's union with God

When you know **whose** you are—beloved child of the eternal God—you discover **who** you are: His masterpiece, being transformed day by day into the image of Christ.

Your Whole Being: A Review

Let's review how each dimension of your being contributes to your True Self:

YOUR BODY (God's Temple)

Designed for worship and service

Tells the truth about your internal state

When surrendered, becomes an instrument of righteousness

Reveals which self is leading through physical presence

YOUR SOUL (Processing Center)

Three control systems: mind, will, emotions

Can be hijacked by fear or surrendered to God

Where wounds are stored but also where healing happens

Processes life through truth or through pain

YOUR SPIRIT (The Anchor)

Already complete in Christ

Where your True Self lives, hidden with Christ in God

God's inner sanctuary where He dwells

Holds you steady when your soul is in turmoil

The Four Selves: Final Understanding

After 29 days, you should now clearly recognize these versions of yourself:

ACTUAL SELF - The honest you, acknowledging both struggle and belovedness. Not perfect, but authentic. This self says: "I'm struggling, AND I'm God's beloved child."

FALSE SELF - The wounded you, operating from fear and using survival strategies. This self says: "I must protect myself because I can't trust anyone—including God."

PRESENTABLE SELF - The curated you, managing impressions to avoid vulnerability. This self says: "If people see the real me, they'll reject me."

TRUE SELF - The Christ-formed you, secure in God's love and naturally expressing His character. This self says: "I am who God says I am, regardless of circumstances."

The goal is not perfection. You'll continue experiencing all four selves at different times. **The goal is awareness**—recognizing which self is showing up and gently redirecting back to your True Self anchored in God's love.

What Has Changed in 29 Days?

Take a moment to honestly assess what's shifted:

Week 1 (Listening):

Can you now distinguish God's voice from other voices more clearly?

Have you developed more soul honesty in prayer?

Are you practicing listening before reacting?

Week 2 (Body):

Do you see your body differently—as God's temple?

Are you more aware of what your body reveals about your internal state?

Have you started caring for your physical self with more grace?

Week 3 (Soul):

Can you identify when your soul's control systems get hijacked?

Are you treating emotions as data rather than directives?

Have you brought specific wounds to God for healing?

Week 4 (Spirit):

Do you experience your spirit as your anchor?

Are you living FROM your spirit instead of FOR it?

Have you felt God's presence in your inner sanctuary?

The Integration of Transformation

Here's what true transformation looks like when body, soul, and spirit work together under the Holy Spirit's leadership:

Your body relaxes from the inside out—peace in your spirit shows in your physical presence

Your soul processes from truth—mind renewed, will surrendered, emotions at rest

Your spirit leads the symphony—anchored in God, conducting all dimensions into harmony

Your True Self emerges naturally—not through striving but through surrender

This is **whole sanctification**—not perfection, but integration. Not performing different versions, but living consistently from who you really are.

Guided Questions for Final Integration

Of everything you've learned in 29 days, what truth has most transformed how you see yourself?

....

....

....

Which of your Four Selves do you now recognize most quickly, and how has that awareness changed your responses?

....

....

....

In which dimension (body, soul, or spirit) have you experienced the most breakthrough, and why?

....

....

....

What specific evidence shows that transformation is happening in your life?

....

....

....

What are you most excited about as you prepare to step into your new beginning tomorrow?

....

....

....

My Thoughts

(Use this space for final reflections on your 29-day journey)

....

....

....

....

Bible Character Reflection

Peter's Complete Transformation – Look at Peter's journey through all four selves:

Before Pentecost:

Actual Self: Honestly struggling—"I don't know the man" (denial)

False Self: Reacting from fear—drew sword, ran away

Presentable Self: Managing image—"I'll never deny You"

True Self: Buried under fear and shame

After Pentecost:

Spirit-filled and anchored in God's love

Body boldly proclaiming Christ despite threats

Soul processing from truth instead of fear

True Self leading—"We ought to obey God rather than men"

Same Peter. Same personality. Same past failures. But now living from his True Self anchored in the Holy Spirit.

This is your destiny too—not perfection, but transformation. Not elimination of struggle, but living from security despite it.

Spiritual Practice of the Day

The 29-Day Testimony (45 minutes)

This is your most important practice—writing your testimony of these 29 days.

Part 1: Where You Started (10 minutes)

Write about Day 1. What was your soul's condition when you began? What questions were you asking? What struggles were you facing?

....

....

....

Part 2: Key Breakthroughs (15 minutes)

Identify 3-5 pivotal moments from the past 29 days:

Week 1 breakthrough: ....

Week 2 breakthrough: ....

Week 3 breakthrough: ....

Week 4 breakthrough: ....

Part 3: Evidence of Change (10 minutes)

List specific, concrete evidence that transformation is happening:

In my thoughts: ....

In my relationships: ....

In my responses: ....

In my awareness: ....

Part 4: Gratitude and Commitment (10 minutes)

Complete these statements:

"Father, I'm grateful for these 29 days because..."

....

"The truth I'm now anchored in is..."

....

"Moving forward, I commit to..."

....

"I declare that I am..."

Prayer of Integration

Father, I stand at the end of 29 days completely overwhelmed by Your faithfulness. You met me exactly where I was—confused about my identity, exhausted from performing, hiding behind masks, driven by wounds.

And You've been so patient. So gentle. So persistent.

Thank You for teaching me to listen—to Your voice and to my own soul's truth. Thank You for helping me see my body as Your temple instead of my enemy. Thank You for healing my damaged soul and restoring what seemed permanently broken. Thank You for revealing that my spirit is my anchor, already complete in Christ.

Most of all, thank You for showing me my True Self—not as something I achieve, but as someone I already am in You. Hidden with Christ in God. Secure. Beloved. Complete.

I'm not the same person who started this journey 29 days ago. Something has fundamentally shifted. I see myself through Your eyes now. I know whose I am, and that's revealing who I am.

As I prepare to step into tomorrow's new beginning, I commit to:

Living FROM my True Self daily

Recognizing when other selves try to take over

Bringing my whole being—body, soul, spirit—under Your loving leadership

Walking worthy of the calling You've given me

I am Yours. Completely. Eternally. Joyfully.

This is not the end of my journey—it's the beginning of living as who I really am.

In Jesus' name, amen.

Daily Declaration

After 29 days of discovery, I now know whose I am: Beloved child of the eternal God. And that reveals who I am: His masterpiece, being transformed daily. Tomorrow, I step into my new beginning.

You are seen. You are loved. You are His.

Your whole being—sanctified and being made whole.

Quote of the Day

"Transformation isn't about becoming someone new—it's about becoming who you've always been beneath the wounds, the masks, and the fear. Your True Self has been waiting. Welcome home."

Day 30 – Your New Beginning: Living From Whose You Are

THE FIRST DAY OF THE REST OF YOUR LIFE

Scripture

"Therefore if any man be in Christ, he is a new creature: old things are passed away; behold, all things are become new."
—2 Corinthians 5:17 (KJV)

"For I know the thoughts that I think toward you, saith the Lord, thoughts of peace, and not of evil, to give you an expected end."
—Jeremiah 29:11 (KJV)

Reflection

Welcome to Day 30—but really, welcome to **Day 1** of living from whose you are.

These past 29 days have been preparation. Discovery. Foundation-building. Healing. Integration. But today—**today you step into the life God has been preparing you for all along.**

This devotional isn't an ending. It's a beginning.

Chapter 12 of *Who Am Eye?* declares: "You are God's masterpiece, being transformed day by day into the image of Christ. The very breath in your lungs is proof that He's not finished with your story yet—the best is yet to come."

Today, you reclaim your identity in Christ and declare who you really are.

From Question to Declaration

You began this journey asking: **"Who Am Eye?"**

You discovered it could only be answered through: **"Whose Am Eye?"**

Now you're ready to **declare** both with confidence:

"I am God's beloved child, chosen before the foundation of the world, redeemed by Christ's blood, sealed by the Holy Spirit, and being transformed daily into His image. I belong completely to the God of all creation, and that settles my identity forever."

This isn't arrogance—it's settled truth. This isn't performance—it's position. This isn't what you hope to become—it's who you already are.

Your Identity Reclaimed

Based on Scripture, here are the non-negotiable truths about your identity that you now embrace:

YOU ARE CHOSEN:

"But ye are a chosen generation, a royal priesthood, an holy nation, a peculiar people" (1 Peter 2:9)

YOU ARE BELOVED:

"Behold, what manner of love the Father hath bestowed upon us, that we should be called the sons of God" (1 John 3:1)

YOU ARE FREE:

"If the Son therefore shall make you free, ye shall be free indeed" (John 8:36)

YOU ARE GOD'S MASTERPIECE:

"For we are his workmanship, created in Christ Jesus unto good works" (Ephesians 2:10)

YOU ARE MORE THAN A CONQUEROR:

"Nay, in all these things we are more than conquerors through him that loved us" (Romans 8:37)

YOU ARE COMPLETE IN CHRIST:

"And ye are complete in him, which is the head of all principality and power" (Colossians 2:10)

These aren't aspirations. These are declarations of present reality.

Living From Your True Self: Practical Daily Steps

Now that you know whose you are and who you are, here's how to live from your True Self daily:

MORNING ANCHORING (5 minutes):

Before checking your phone, place your hand on your heart and say out loud

"I am God's beloved child. I belong to Him completely."

"Today I choose to live from my True Self—secure, loved, free."

"Holy Spirit, lead my body, soul, and spirit today."

THROUGHOUT THE DAY:

When triggered: Pause. "Which self wants to respond? Let my True Self lead."

When anxious: Breathe. "My spirit is anchored in God's unchanging love."

When performing: Stop. "I don't need to earn what I already have."

When hiding: Risk. "I can be authentic because I'm already accepted."

EVENING REFLECTION (5 minutes): Ask yourself the following questions -

"Where did I experience my True Self today?" (Celebrate)

"Where did other selves take over?" (Grace, not shame)

"What did I learn about living from whose I am?" (Growth)

Your Four Selves: The Path Forward

You'll continue experiencing all four selves. That's normal. Here's how to navigate them from your new understanding:

When ACTUAL SELF shows up (struggling but honest):
Embrace it. "I'm struggling AND I'm God's beloved. Both are true."

When FALSE SELF emerges (wounded and reactive):
Recognize it. "That's my wound talking, not my True Self. I choose healing."

When PRESENTABLE SELF appears (performing and hiding):
Redirect it. "I don't need this mask. I'm already accepted completely."

When TRUE SELF leads (secure and authentic):
Celebrate it. "This is who I really am. This is living from whose I am."

The goal isn't perfection—it's awareness and redirection. You're learning to live from your True Self more consistently, extending grace when other selves surface.

The Three Questions for Your Journey Forward

As you move beyond these 30 days, three questions will guide you:

1. "Which self is showing up right now?"
(Awareness is the first step to transformation)

2. "What is my soul processing, and is it processing from truth or from wounds?"
(Soul care requires ongoing attention)

3. "Am I living FROM my spirit's security or FOR my spirit's perfection?"
(Rest vs. striving changes everything)

These simple questions, asked regularly, prayerfully will keep you anchored in God's truth.

Your New Beginning Starts Now

Here's what I want you to understand as you close this devotional and step into your new beginning:

You are not the same person who started this journey 30 days ago. Something fundamental has shifted. My prayer is that you see yourself differently, you understand your worth and you recognize the voices of lies. You know whose you are.

You will still struggle. There will be days when your False Self dominates. Times when your Presentable Self exhausts you. Moments when you forget everything you've learned. That's not failure—that's being human in the "not yet" of transformation.

Your True Self is secure. No matter which version shows up on the surface, your True Self remains anchored in God's love, hidden with Christ, complete in Him. The storm doesn't change the anchor's hold.

The best is yet to come. God isn't finished with your story. Every day is an opportunity to live more consistently from your True Self. Every struggle is an invitation to deeper surrender. Every wound is a doorway to greater healing.

Guided Questions for Your New Beginning

How do you want to be different one year from today because of what you've learned in these 30 days?

....

....

....

What specific practice from this devotional will you continue as part of your daily spiritual formation?

....

....

....

Who in your life needs to hear that they're beloved, chosen, and complete in Christ—and how will you share your story with them?

....

....

....

Complete this sentence: "Because I now know whose I am, I will..."

....

....

....

My Final Thoughts

(Use this space for your personal declaration and commitment)

....

....

....

....

Bible Character Reflection

Paul's Declaration – After his transformation, Paul lived from this settled identity:

"For I am persuaded, that neither death, nor life, nor angels, nor principalities, nor powers, nor things present, nor things to come, Nor height, nor depth, nor any other creature, shall be able to separate us from the love of God, which is in Christ Jesus our Lord" (Romans 8:38-39).

Paul knew **whose** he was. Nothing could change that. From that security, he lived boldly, loved radically, served sacrificially, and suffered without bitterness.

Like Paul, your identity is settled. Now live from that unshakeable foundation.

Spiritual Practice of the Day

Your Personal Identity Declaration (30 minutes)

Using everything you've learned, write your personal identity declaration. Make it specific, biblical, and authentic to your journey.

Template:

"I, [your name], declare that I am [biblical identity truths].

I belong to [who God is to you].

My True Self is [description of who you are in Christ].

I renounce [specific lies you're breaking agreement with].

I embrace [specific truths you're choosing to believe].

Moving forward, I commit to [specific daily practices].

I declare this in faith, knowing that [God's faithfulness statement].

Signed: _____________ Date: _____________"

Write your full declaration here:

....

....

....

....

....

....

Prayer for Your New Beginning

Father, I stand at the threshold of my new beginning, overwhelmed with gratitude for these 30 days.

Thank You for meeting me in my confusion and revealing truth. Thank You for patience with my resistance and persistence in my transformation. Thank You for not giving up on me when I wanted to give up on myself.

I declare today: **I know whose I am.**

I am Yours—chosen before the foundation of the world, redeemed by Christ's blood, sealed by Your Spirit, and being transformed daily into Your image.

Because I know whose I am, I now know who I am:

Your beloved child, not an orphan

Your masterpiece, not a mistake

Your temple, not a wasteland

Your ambassador, not a reject

Your joy, not Your burden

My True Self is anchored in these truths. When other versions surface—and they will—I'll recognize them, extend grace, and redirect to who I really am.

As I step into this new beginning:

Help me live FROM my spirit's security, not FOR spiritual perfection

Teach me to recognize which self is leading and gently redirect

Give me courage to be authentic instead of hiding behind masks

Grant me wisdom to process my soul through truth instead of wounds

Fill me with awareness of Your presence in my inner sanctuary

I'm done asking "Who am I?" in desperation. I'm declaring "I am Yours" with confidence.

This is my new beginning. The first day of living from whose I am.

In Jesus' name, amen.

Daily Declaration

After 30 days, I declare: I know whose I am—beloved child of the eternal God. I know who I am—His masterpiece being transformed daily. I know where I live—hidden with Christ in God. Today is not an ending. Today is my new beginning.

You are seen. You are loved. You are His.

Now go live like you believe it.

Quote of the Day

"You've spent 30 days discovering whose you are. Now spend the rest of your life living from that unshakeable truth. Your True Self has been waiting for this moment. Welcome to your new beginning."

Where You Go From Here

CONTINUE THE PRACTICES:

CONTINUE THE PRACTICES:

Morning identity anchoring

Midday "which self" check-ins

Evening reflection and grace

Weekly soul care

CONNECT WITH COMMUNITY: Visit www.learnlivehopejourney.info for:

Additional resources

Community support

Ongoing formation tools

SHARE YOUR STORY: Someone in your life needs to hear that transformation is possible. Your testimony matters. Your journey can become their hope.

COMPANION RESOURCES:

"Who Am Eye? - Identity Forming Program" for deeper work

"Whose Am Eye?" for mission and purpose discovery

Monthly devotionals for ongoing formation

MOST IMPORTANTLY: Remember this: You are not who your wounds say you are. You are not who your fear says you are. You are not who your performance says you are.

You are who God says you are.

And He says: "Beloved. Chosen. Free. Mine."

Now go live from that truth.

You've completed the 30-day journey. Your transformation continues. Welcome to the beginning of everything.

Appendix A

Daily Practice Guide Appendix

<u>Morning Practices (5-10 minutes)</u>

Identity Anchoring Routine

Time: 5 minutes

Before checking your phone, place your hand on your heart

Speak aloud: "I am God's beloved child. I belong to Him completely."

Declare: "Today I choose to live from my True Self—secure, loved, free."

Pray: "Holy Spirit, lead my body, soul, and spirit today."

<u>Body Awareness Check</u>

Time: 2 minutes

Take three deep breaths

Notice where you're holding tension

Stretch or move gently

Thank God for His temple—your body

<u>Scripture Declaration</u>

Time: 3 minutes

Choose one verse from Appendix B and:

Read it aloud

Personalize it (replace "you" with "I")

Declare it over your identity

Midday Practices (3-5 minutes)

The "Which Self" Check-In

Set 2-3 alarms throughout your day

When the alarm sounds, pause and ask:

Body Check: Where am I holding tension?

Soul Check: What thoughts are on repeat? Are they true?

Spirit Check: Do I feel connected to God right now?

Self Check: Which version of me is leading right now?

If you notice hijacking or protective patterns:

Recognize it without judgment

Pause before reacting

Reconnect with Holy Spirit

Redirect from your True Self

Three-Breath Reset

When triggered or anxious:

Breath 1: "My spirit is anchored in God's love"

Breath 2: "My True Self is secure in Christ"

Breath 3: "I choose to respond from peace, not fear"

Evening Practices (10-15 minutes)

Daily Reflection Questions

Time: 7 minutes

Journal brief answers to these three questions:

Where did I experience my True Self today? (Celebrate this)

Where did other selves take over? (Extend grace, not shame)

What did I learn about living from whose I am? (Note growth)

Soul Conversation

Time: 5 minutes

Talk TO your soul like David did:

"O my soul, what did you process today?"

"What are you feeling? What are you needing?"

Then redirect: "Hope in God, for I shall again praise Him"

Gratitude and Release

Time: 3 minutes

Thank God for three specific things from today

Release any burdens: "Father, I give You [specific worry]"

Rest declaration: "I am Yours. You hold my tomorrow."

Weekly Practices (15-30 minutes)

Sunday Evening: Weekly Identity Review

Time: 20 minutes

Which of my Four Selves showed up most this week?

What patterns am I noticing in my reactions?

How can I live more from my True Self next week?

What is God teaching me about whose I am?

The Four-Step Soul Care Process

When you notice a recurring wound or trigger:

Step 1: Name the wound specifically (3 min)

"This is what happened..."

"This is how it damaged my soul..."

Step 2: Recognize the pattern (3 min)

"Because of this wound, I developed this protective strategy..."

Step 3: Renounce the lie (3 min)

"I renounce the lie that..."

"I break agreement with this false belief..."

Step 4: Receive God's truth (6 min)

"Father, what is Your truth about this wound?"

"I receive Your love specifically into this broken place..."

Scripture Memory Practice

Time: 10 minutes

Choose one verse from Appendix B to memorize this week

Write it on a card

Read it aloud morning and evening

Speak it over yourself when triggered

Monthly Practices (30-60 minutes)

Monthly Soul Inventory

Last Sunday of each month:

Complete these assessments:

Body Assessment:

How well am I caring for God's temple?

What is my body telling me about my internal state?

Do I need more rest? Movement? Nourishment?

Soul Assessment:

Which control system (mind, will, emotions) needs attention?

What wounds still hijack my processing?

Am I bringing my soul to the Healer regularly?

Spirit Assessment:

Am I living FROM my spirit or FOR my spirit?

How connected do I feel to my True Self?

Do I experience my spirit as God's sanctuary?

The Container Prayer

Time: 15 minutes

Hold an empty cup/bowl and pray through:

Acknowledge damage (5 min): "Father, my soul's container was damaged by..."

Invite restoration (5 min): "Seal every crack with Christ's blood..."

Receive filling (5 min): "Fill me with Your presence..."

As-Needed Practices

When Emotions Overwhelm

The Emotion Translation Exercise (10 minutes)

Name the emotion: What am I feeling? (Don't spiritualize yet)

What data is it giving?: What is this emotion trying to tell me?

Which self is interpreting?: False? Presentable? True?

Pray: "Father, this emotion is data. Show me how to respond from my True Self."

When Identity Feels Shaky

The Anchor Meditation (15 minutes)

Visualize the storm (3 min): Acknowledge what's shaking you

Feel the anchor (7 min): Picture your spirit anchored in God's love

Trust the hold (5 min): "My True Self is unreachable by storms"

When You Need to Forgive

The Forgiveness Prayer (20 minutes)

Name the wound honestly before God

Acknowledge the impact on your soul

Choose to forgive: "I forgive [person] for [specific action]"

Release your right to revenge or repayment

Invite God's healing into that specific place

Building Sustainable Habits

Start Small

Week 1-2: Morning anchoring only (5 min)

Week 3-4: Add midday check-ins (3 min)

Week 5-6: Add evening reflection (10 min)

Week 7+: Add weekly/monthly practices

Be Consistent, Not Perfect

Missing a day doesn't mean failure

Grace over guilt—always

Progress over perfection

Small daily steps create lasting change

Remember

These practices are **tools for grace**, not tasks for performance. They help you:

Live FROM your True Self (not work FOR acceptance)

Stay anchored in whose you are (not earn who you are)

Process your soul with God (not manage it alone)

"Being confident of this very thing, that he which hath begun a good work in you will perform it until the day of Jesus Christ" (Philippians 1:6).

Appendix B

Scripture Memory Verses

Verses for Identity Formation

Who You Are in Christ

1 Peter 2:9 (KJV) "But ye are a chosen generation, a royal priesthood, an holy nation, a peculiar people; that ye should shew forth the praises of him who hath called you out of darkness into his marvellous light."

2 Corinthians 5:17 (KJV) "Therefore if any man be in Christ, he is a new creature: old things are passed away; behold, all things are become new."

Ephesians 2:10 (KJV) "For we are his workmanship, created in Christ Jesus unto good works, which God hath before ordained that we should walk in them."

1 John 3:1 (KJV) "Behold, what manner of love the Father hath bestowed upon us, that we should be called the sons of God: therefore the world knoweth us not, because it knew him not."

Colossians 3:3 (KJV) "For ye are dead, and your life is hid with Christ in God."

Verses for Body (God's Temple)

1 Corinthians 6:19-20 (KJV) "What? know ye not that your body is the temple of the Holy Ghost which is in you, which ye have of God, and ye are not your own? For ye are bought with a price: therefore glorify God in your body, and in your spirit, which are God's."

Romans 12:1 (KJV) "I beseech you therefore, brethren, by the mercies of God, that ye present your bodies a living sacrifice, holy, acceptable unto God, which is your reasonable service."

Psalm 139:14 (KJV) "I will praise thee; for I am fearfully and wonderfully made: marvellous are thy works; and that my soul knoweth right well."

Verses for Soul (Processing Center)

Romans 12:2 (KJV) "And be not conformed to this world: but be ye transformed by the renewing of your mind, that ye may prove what is that good, and acceptable, and perfect, will of God."

Psalm 42:5 (KJV) "Why art thou cast down, O my soul? and why art thou disquieted in me? hope thou in God: for I shall yet praise him for the help of his countenance."

Philippians 2:13 (KJV) "For it is God which worketh in you both to will and to do of his good pleasure."

Psalm 51:10 (KJV) "Create in me a clean heart, O God; and renew a right spirit within me."

Psalm 147:3 (KJV) "He healeth the broken in heart, and bindeth up their wounds."

Verses for Spirit (The Anchor)

1 Corinthians 6:17 (KJV) "But he that is joined unto the Lord is one spirit."

Proverbs 20:27 (KJV) "The spirit of man is the candle of the Lord, searching all the inward parts of the belly."

Galatians 2:20 (KJV) "I am crucified with Christ: nevertheless I live; yet not I, but Christ liveth in me: and the life which I now live in the flesh I live by the faith of the Son of God, who loved me, and gave himself for me."

Hebrews 4:9-10 (KJV) "There remaineth therefore a rest to the people of God. For he that is entered into his rest, he also hath ceased from his own works, as God did from his."

Verses for Living FROM Your True Self

Galatians 3:3 (KJV) "Are ye so foolish? having begun in the Spirit, are ye now made perfect by the flesh?"

Ephesians 4:1 (KJV) "I therefore, the prisoner of the Lord, beseech you that ye walk worthy of the vocation wherewith ye are called."

Philippians 3:12 (KJV) "Not as though I had already attained, either were already perfect: but I follow after, if that I may apprehend that for which also I am apprehended of Christ Jesus."

Philippians 1:6 (KJV) "Being confident of this very thing, that he which hath begun a good work in you will perform it until the day of Jesus Christ."

Verses for When Different Selves Emerge

When Your Actual Self Struggles

2 Corinthians 12:9 (KJV) "And he said unto me, My grace is sufficient for thee: for my strength is made perfect in weakness. Most gladly therefore will I rather glory in my infirmities, that the power of Christ may rest upon me."

Romans 8:26 (KJV) "Likewise the Spirit also helpeth our infirmities: for we know not what we should pray for as we ought: but the Spirit itself maketh intercession for us with groanings which cannot be uttered."

When Your False Self Reacts

2 Timothy 1:7 (KJV) "For God hath not given us the spirit of fear; but of power, and of love, and of a sound mind."

Isaiah 43:2 (KJV) "When thou passest through the waters, I will be with thee; and through the rivers, they shall not overflow thee: when thou walkest through the fire, thou shalt not be burned; neither shall the flame kindle upon thee."

When Your Presentable Self Performs

Galatians 1:10 (KJV) "For do I now persuade men, or God? or do I seek to please men? for if I yet pleased men, I should not be the servant of Christ."

1 Samuel 16:7 (KJV) "But the Lord said unto Samuel, Look not on his countenance, or on the height of his stature; because I have refused him: for the Lord seeth not as man seeth; for man looketh on the outward appearance, but the Lord looketh on the heart."

When Your True Self Leads

Colossians 2:10 (KJV) "And ye are complete in him, which is the head of all principality and power."

Romans 8:37 (KJV) "Nay, in all these things we are more than conquerors through him that loved us."

Verses for Specific Situations

When Anxious or Fearful

Philippians 4:6-7 (KJV) "Be careful for nothing; but in every thing by prayer and supplication with thanksgiving let your requests be made known unto God. And the peace of God, which passeth all understanding, shall keep your hearts and minds through Christ Jesus."

Isaiah 41:10 (KJV) "Fear thou not; for I am with thee: be not dismayed; for I am thy God: I will strengthen thee; yea, I will help thee; yea, I will uphold thee with the right hand of my righteousness."

When Ashamed or Condemned

Romans 8:1 (KJV) "There is therefore now no condemnation to them which are in Christ Jesus, who walk not after the flesh, but after the Spirit."

Psalm 34:5 (KJV) "They looked unto him, and were lightened: and their faces were not ashamed."

When Doubting Your Worth

Jeremiah 31:3 (KJV) "The Lord hath appeared of old unto me, saying, Yea, I have loved thee with an everlasting love: therefore with lovingkindness have I drawn thee."

Zephaniah 3:17 (KJV) "The Lord thy God in the midst of thee is mighty; he will save, he will rejoice over thee with joy; he will rest in his love, he will joy over thee with singing."

When Needing Transformation

1 John 3:2 (KJV) "Beloved, now are we the sons of God, and it doth not yet appear what we shall be: but we know that, when he shall appear, we shall be like him; for we shall see him as he is."

Philippians 3:20-21 (KJV) "For our conversation is in heaven; from whence also we look for the Saviour, the Lord Jesus Christ: Who shall change our vile body, that it may be fashioned like unto his glorious body."

When Unable to Forgive

Ephesians 4:32 (KJV) "And be ye kind one to another, tenderhearted, forgiving one another, even as God for Christ's sake hath forgiven you."

Matthew 6:14-15 (KJV) "For if ye forgive men their trespasses, your heavenly Father will also forgive you: But if ye forgive not men their trespasses, neither will your Father forgive your trespasses."

Monthly Memory Plan

Month 1: Ephesians 2:10 (Identity as God's masterpiece)
Month 2: 1 Corinthians 6:19-20 (Body as temple)
Month 3: Romans 12:2 (Soul transformation)
Month 4: Galatians 2:20 (Spirit anchored in Christ)
Month 5: 2 Corinthians 5:17 (New creation)
Month 6: Romans 8:37 (More than conqueror)
Month 7: Colossians 3:3 (Hidden with Christ)
Month 8: Philippians 1:6 (God completes His work)
Month 9: 1 Peter 2:9 (Chosen generation)
Month 10: 2 Timothy 1:7 (Not given spirit of fear)
Month 11: Isaiah 43:2 (God's presence in trials)
Month 12: 1 John 3:1 (Called sons of God)

Tip for Memorization:

Write the verse on a card

Read it aloud 3 times each morning

Repeat it throughout the day when waiting (traffic, lines, etc.)

Speak it over yourself when the situation it addresses arises

By day 7, you'll have it memorized

Online Resources

Learn Live Hope Journey Ministry

Website: www.learnlivehopejourney.info
Email: johangreenlearnlivehopejourney.com

For Ongoing Support:

Podcast: Dr. Johan Green (available on major podcast platforms)

Weekly live Q&A sessions on identity formation

Recorded teachings and sermons

Spiritual formation resources

YouTube: https://www.youtube.com/@drjohangreen

Additional Programs:

Who Am Eye? - Identity Forming Program (12-week comprehensive curriculum)

Devotional Series (ongoing spiritual formation)

Community Groups (online and local chapters)

Upcoming Resources:

Whose Am Eye? - Companion book exploring mission and purpose

Who Am Eye? - Devotionals

Leading from His Presence - For those in leadership

Divorced Again - Grace-filled guidance for relationship loss / struggles and healing

Disqualified - Overcoming feelings of disqualification

Social Media:

Connect with our growing community for daily encouragement and identity-focused content.

For Speaking Engagements or Ministry Inquiries:

Email: johangreenlearnlivehopejourney.com

Note to Readers:

Whether you're part of a local church community or walking this path individually, you're never alone in your transformation journey. The Learn Live Hope Journey family is committed to supporting believers in discovering and living from their True Self in Christ.

We invite you to connect, share your story, and join others who are learning to answer "Who Am Eye?" by first knowing "Whose Am Eye?"

Companion Book

This 30-day devotional is designed as a companion resource to:

Who Am Eye? The Question That Is Only 'Whose Am Eye?'

by Dr. Johan Green

Published by Learn Live Hope Journey LLC

For the complete identity formation journey, we recommend reading the full book alongside this devotional.

Disclaimer

This devotional is provided for educational and spiritual growth purposes only within a Christian framework. This content represents biblical principles and pastoral guidance, not psychological counseling, mental health treatment, or professional therapy.

If you are experiencing mental health concerns, persistent depression, anxiety, thoughts of self-harm, or psychological distress, please seek help from qualified licensed mental health professionals. This devotional is intended to support your spiritual journey alongside, not in place of, appropriate professional care when needed.

The author and publisher are not liable for any misuse or misinterpretation of the content provided in this devotional.

Bibliography

Books Referenced and Recommended

Allender, Dan B. *The Healing Path: How the Hurts in Your Past Can Lead You to a More Abundant Life.* Colorado Springs: WaterBrook Press, 2000.

Anderson, Neil T. *Victory Over the Darkness: Realizing the Power of Your Identity in Christ.* Ventura, CA: Regal Books, 2000.

Bonhoeffer, Dietrich. *Life Together: The Classic Exploration of Christian Community.* New York: HarperOne, 1954.

Chan, Edmund. *The Intentional Disciple: Making Disciples the Jesus Way.* Singapore: Covenant Evangelical Free Church, 2013.

Gaylin, Willard. *Feelings: Our Vital Signs.* New York: Harper & Row, 1979.

Green, Johan. *Who Am Eye? The Question That Is Only 'Whose Am Eye?'* Learn Live Hope Journey LLC, 2024.

Heifetz, Ronald A. *Leadership Without Easy Answers.* Cambridge, MA: Harvard University Press, 1994.

Kaufman, Gershen. *Shame: The Power of Caring.* 3rd ed. Rochester, VT: Schenkman Books, 1992.

Lewis, C.S. *The Problem of Pain.* New York: Macmillan, 1962.

Manning, Brennan. *Abba's Child: The Cry of the Heart for Intimate Belonging.* Colorado Springs: NavPress, 1994.

Mulholland, M. Robert Jr. *Invitation to a Journey: A Road Map for*

Spiritual Formation. Downers Grove, IL: InterVarsity Press, 1993.

Nee, Watchman. *The Spiritual Man.* 3 vols. New York: Christian Fellowship Publishers, 1968.

Nouwen, Henri J.M. *Life of the Beloved: Spiritual Living in a Secular World.* New York: Crossroad Publishing, 1992.

Reimer, Rob. *Soul Care: 7 Transformational Principles for a Healthy Soul.* Franklin, TN: Carpenter's Son Publishing, 2016.

Scazzero, Peter. *Emotionally Healthy Spirituality: It's Impossible to Be Spiritually Mature While Remaining Emotionally Immature.* Grand Rapids: Zondervan, 2017.

Smedes, Lewis B. *Shame and Grace: Healing the Shame We Don't Deserve.* New York: HarperOne, 1993.

Willard, Dallas. *Renovation of the Heart: Putting On the Character of Christ.* Colorado Springs: NavPress, 2002.